IMAGES
*of America*

# NESHANIC AND
# NESHANIC STATION

*On the Cover:* The bridge over the south branch of the Raritan at Neshanic was ordered from a catalogue from the Berlin Bridge Company of Connecticut. The bridge was erected in 1896, and it is pictured here about 1906. Only 50 of these bridges still remain of the more than 1,000 constructed. The bridge is listed on the National Register of Historic Places as part of Hillsborough's Neshanic Mills Historical District. (Photograph courtesy of Harry Smith.)

# IMAGES of America
# NESHANIC AND NESHANIC STATION

Neshanic Station Historical Society

ARCADIA
PUBLISHING

Copyright © 1999 by Neshanic Station Historical Society
ISBN 9781531600914

Published by Arcadia Publishing
Charleston, South Carolina

Library of Congress Catalog Card Number: Applied For.

For all general information contact Arcadia Publishing at:
Telephone 843-853-2070
Fax 843-853-0044
E-mail sales@arcadiapublishing.com
For customer service and orders:
Toll-Free 1-888-313-2665

Visit us on the Internet at www.arcadiapublishing.com

This view of Shadowlawn shows the front porch and south-side entrance facing the Central Railroad of New Jersey. Mr. John G. Schenck, the original resident of Shadowlawn, helped to bring the railroad to the area. The home, started in 1858, had its frame blown down in a storm during the Civil War and was completed at the end of the war. (Photograph courtesy of Branchburg Township Historical Society.)

# Contents

| | | |
|---|---|---|
| Acknowledgments | | 6 |
| Introduction | | 7 |
| 1. | Neshanic of Hillsborough | 9 |
| 2. | Neshanic Station of Branchburg | 19 |
| 3. | Village Churches | 41 |
| 4. | Railroads | 57 |
| 5. | Neshanic Volunteer Fire Company | 65 |
| 6. | Agriculture | 75 |
| 7. | Commerce and Industry | 83 |
| 8. | Recreation, Leisure, and Community Activities | 113 |

# ACKNOWLEDGMENTS

We thank everyone who offered pictures, stories, ideas, and information. Each and every contribution has added to the quality of this book. A heartfelt thanks to Laurence B. Lane for sharing a large portion of the Lane family glass negatives, and to Paul Kurzenberger for sharing postcards of our area and for putting us in touch with Robert Yuell, who also shared his postcard collection. Thanks to William Schleicher and to Robert Bouwman for their advice.

This project was funded in part by a grant from the Somerset County Cultural & Heritage Commission and Forbes, Inc.

Regarding errors and omissions, we admit to not being perfect and we were limited to the number of pages seen within.

The Neshanic Station Historical Society: Joe Hoff, president; G.W. "Bill" Amerman; Alma Quick Deak; Amy Fenwick Frank; Jim Grill; Robert Guterl; Eric and Traci Gorky; Karen Hoff; Frieda Miller; Ted and Heidi Schlatter Saunders; and Bob and Kathie Schwarz.

This aerial view of the historic Elm Street Bridge and the Lehigh Valley Railroad Dual Track Bridge was taken by A. Schenck Bergen. (Unpublished work, c. 1998; courtesy of Olivia Cutler.)

# INTRODUCTION

After the land grants of the late 17th century, the areas that would become Branchburg and Hillsborough Townships gradually became settled. While Hillsborough was organized in 1745, Branchburg (originally a part of Bridgewater Township) was not organized until 1845. Many of those coming to the area after the Revolutionary War were veterans. Amwell Road was a main thoroughfare from the earliest days, and the village of Neshanic was formed around the traffic that passed through. The name is said to have originated from the name for the area, which was based on the curved South Branch of the Raritan River that was seen to resemble the neck of a goose. During this period, the population in the area grew sufficiently to merit the organization of the Reformed Dutch Church of Neshanic in 1752. One of the founders of the Reformed Church was Reverend John Frelinghuysen, ancestor of Rodney Frelinghuysen, a current member of Congress. The first mill in the area was built at about 1770, at or near the end of Mill Lane. A second mill replaced it in 1810, not far away from the first, toward the village of Neshanic. A final replacement built on the site is now a private residence. While crossings over the South Branch of the Raritan River were originally made at a ford, a listing of the bridges in existence in Somerset County in 1797 includes a bridge at New Shannick (Snell's History of Hunterdon and Somerset Counties).

In 1860, much of the present village of Neshanic Station was still a part of one of the area's larger farms, belonging to John Schenck. His home, Shadowlawn (which still stands), was under construction in 1860 when the frame apparently was blown down in a storm. It was completed during the Civil War. Local folklore says that the large trees in front of the house were being planted on the day that President Lincoln was shot. Schenck was a New Jersey assemblyman (1861–1865 and 1872–1874), a state senator (1879–1881), and a state railroad commissioner. He is credited with bringing at least one of the two railroads to Neshanic Station. The South Branch Railroad, a part of the Central Railroad of New Jersey that extended from Flemington to Somerville, was chartered in 1870, and completed soon after. According to Snell, it had stations at "Somerville (connecting with the main line, east and west), Ricefield, Flaggtown, Neshanic, Three Bridges, and Flemington." It was the two railroads that gave the village of Neshanic Station its identity. Previously, the village of Neshanic was known as "Upper Neshanic," while the village of Neshanic Station was known as "Lower Neshanic." The two villages were linked by a road, named "Main Street."

One interesting story about the construction of the Lehigh Valley Railroad embankment has emerged more than once. Apparently, the railroad was originally erected on a wooden trestle, which was replaced with the present earth embankment. A landslide during the course of construction was blamed for the death of a worker who allegedly perished with his mules and wagon. Since it was clear that he had died, his body was left and the work continued with a minimum of delay. The story is consistent with the reputation of the railroads as cruel spoilers during that period. Other stories about Union soldiers during the Civil War bivouacking on the field down from Orville Shurts's feed mill (now the Neshanic Garden Center) and being fed from produce purchased locally are also believable.

A map on file at the Somerset County Clerk's office shows Neshanic Station, in 1873, with the tracks of the Central Railroad, the Easton and Amboy Railroad (later leased and operated by the Lehigh Valley Railroad), the Central Railroad station, and a cluster of homes at the intersection of Main Street and Elm Street. Snell's History of Hunterdon and Somerset Counties describes the village of Neshanic in 1881, as containing "one Reformed (Dutch) church, a hotel (temperance), a district school, two stores and some 25 dwellings. About ten more are at Neshanic Station."

At the end of the 19th century, Neshanic Station reached its commercial high point, and the village of Neshanic gradually lost its commercial identity. The area had become an established fruit growing region, and older lifetime residents recall being told of the long lines of wagons laden with fruit waiting to be loaded onto freight cars bound for the cities. As commerce in the area grew, these railroads came to support two passenger stations, two freight stations, two creameries, two lumber yards, as many as four general stores, a blacksmith's shop, a hotel, a butcher shop, a silver shop, saddlery, and a fruit evaporating company founded by John Schenck.

The fruit trees, which for a time provided the major source of income for the farmers in the area, died early in this century after contracting a mysterious blight. This apparently brought about the failure of the fruit evaporating business operated by John Schenck. After his bankruptcy, the residential nature of the village was enlarged by the construction of homes on the county's first recorded subdivision, "Villa Sites," filed in 1875. Many of the homes on those lots were built in the first ten years of the 20th century, with the sale of lots by the trustees of John G. Schenck continuing after his death in 1905. It was apparently a matter of family honor that the investors in the failed fruit evaporating business were to be paid in full, and tradition has it that they were.

A major fire in 1910 destroyed the lumber yard, the hotel, and a number of other buildings and stores. Only the hotel and lumber yard were rebuilt. Stories about Presidents Theodore Roosevelt, Woodrow Wilson, and others giving short speeches from the rear of a train or from the front porch of the Methodist church are likely to be true since campaigning by railroad was common during this period. Also during this period, there was an icehouse by the river, and the millpond produced a regular supply of ice for local residents and neighboring farms. Electricity came to the village in 1922, and a volunteer fire company was started in 1928. There were plenty of summer baseball games and even some local theatrical productions in the fire company hall, which was built with a stage.

As the 20th century progressed, Neshanic Station's commerce started to decline as the four general stores gradually dwindled to one. Passenger service to and from Neshanic Station on the Central Jersey Railroad ended in 1953. Freight service continued for a few years on the Central Jersey line, but finally ended on this line with the bankruptcy of the Central Jersey Railroad in the 1970s, the ultimate sale of its properties, and even its right of way. By the 1960s, the J.S. Amerman lumber yard, Orville Shurts's feed store, the J.S. Covert John Deere dealership, Hoff's Electric, the post office (since relocated to a larger modern facility), a bar and restaurant in the old hotel, the volunteer fire company, and one general store remained.

Many current residents have lifelong links to the villages. Orville Shurts operated the feed mill that his father founded. When his grandfather, Garrett Stryker Shurts, died suddenly in 1910 on his farm, his widow, Mary Lavina Shurts, sold the family farm and built her home in Neshanic Station so that she could be near her son, Lester Shurts. In 1898, he had started the feed store business that his son Orville eventually took over in 1898. Another resident, Robert May, came here with his father, the first pastor of the Neshanic Methodist Church. It was his father who successfully approached tobacco magnate James B. Duke for funds to aid in the building of that church. G.W. "Bill" Amerman, a descendant of the earliest settlers of the area, operated the local lumber yard until recently and was the major contributor to this book. Laurence B. Lane's father operated the general store in the village of Neshanic until it was destroyed by fire.

Today, Neshanic and Neshanic Station are almost entirely residential communities, but the pictures in this book will give a glimpse of a very different time for these villages. Conrail still makes regular freight runs on the Lehigh tracks, and the hills still ring with the sounds of train whistles. While much of the commerce is gone, the sense of community remains.

# One
# Neshanic of Hillsborough

The Neshanic Hotel (724 Amwell Road) appears on the Hillsborough Registry directly after the Reformed Church, built in 1752. The inn and tavern seem to have co-existed, since the inn was listed as a temperance inn in 1873. The post road from New Brunswick to Flemington was established by Congress in early 1838, and the Amwell Stage Line started in that year. The line made trips three times a week between Johines Hotel, in New Brunswick, and Mahlon C. Harts, in Flemington, via Millstone, Flagtown, Shannock (Neshanic), Clover Hill, and Reaville. (Photograph courtesy of L.B. Lane.)

A triple horse team hitch is shown, in this 1908 postcard, meeting another wagon east of Neshanic Reformed Church on Amwell Road. Note the stovepipe on the church roof. Stoves served in all four corners of the church prior to the furnace installation. (Photograph courtesy of Paul Kurzenberger.)

This view looking west toward Neshanic Station depicts the home of Ace and Charles Hall on the right. The barn is gone, but the house is still seen today with an addition on the west side (1144 River Road). (Photograph courtesy of L.B. Lane.)

This unknown person is standing next to an artesian well with a dipping pail beam c. 1900, located near the foot of Zion Road. (Photograph courtesy of L.B. Lane.)

This c. 1900 Garroway Reed photo postcard shows Amwell Road looking west (on the right) and Zion Road (on the left). (Photograph courtesy of L.B. Lane.)

This c. 1900 image presents a view of Neshanic, along Amwell Road, as seen from the McGill Farm (721 Amwell Road), also known as DuBois or Sebring Farm. Note the buggy on the road. (Photograph courtesy of L.B. Lane.)

On the right can be seen the original home of Esther Karsner (deceased) off of Zion Road, overlooking the village of Neshanic. (Photograph courtesy of L.B. Lane.)

A wood-fired, steam-powered sawmill is shown in this pre-1900 photograph sawing oak logs from the Sourland Mountains. Horse-drawn wagons and sleds brought the logs down to the roadside below the Neshanic Church, seen in the background. (Photograph courtesy of L.B. Lane.)

A sawyer is shown in this photograph standing by the running blade. Railroad ties are waiting to be cut to length, possibly for the Central Railroad of New Jersey South Branch Line, which ran through Neshanic Station. (Photograph courtesy of L.B. Lane.)

This photograph, taken in 1919, illustrates the home of Dr. John E. Andersen (1143 River Road), alongside the Neshanic Reformed Church, with his Model T parked in front. Dr. Andersen started his practice here in 1874, and he served the community for half a century. (Photograph courtesy of L.B. Lane.)

Dr. John E. Andersen and family are represented in this photograph on the front porch of their home. Later, this was the home and office of Dr. S.H. Husted, who joined with Dr. Andersen just prior to his retirement. (Photograph courtesy of Dan Bassuk.)

Dr. Andersen is shown here on Amwell Road with his pet hunting dog in 1919. (Photograph courtesy of L.B. Lane.)

J.C. Lane Jr. is shown here with L.B. Lane (on bicycle seat) on Amwell Road in 1919. (Photograph courtesy of L.B. Lane.)

Station Road is shown in this c. 1912 photo postcard looking from "Old Neshanic" toward Neshanic Station. Dr. Andersen's dog and daughter are in the foreground by the bridge. (Courtesy of Robert Yuell.)

Elizabeth Lane, Laura Lane, and John C. Lane are seen here enjoying Sunday dinner at home prior to electricity in 1919. Mr. Lane operated the country corner store next to the Andersens' home. (Photograph courtesy of L.B. Lane.)

In this c. 1900 winter scene, John Lane (in the center with a shovel) is trying to clear the road in front of his store with the help of some neighbors. (Photograph courtesy of L.B. Lane.)

This c. 1900 photograph shows the Neshanic School. This one-room school was later used by the Neshanic Reformed Church for Sunday school and now forms the central part of Brookside Hall. Snell's History of Somerset County records that the Neshanic School "probably dates back to 1750." In 1880, it was one of 14 schools in Hillsborough Township. The following statistics are recorded for the year ending August 31, 1879: total received from all sources for public school purposes, $1,183.08; present value of the school property, $25; children of school age residing in the district, 111; average number of months the school was kept open, 9; children enrolled in school register during the year, 65; seating capacity, 20. (Photograph courtesy of L.B. Lane.)

This photograph represents the class of 1913 at the Neshanic School. (Photograph courtesy of L.B. Lane.)

Neshanic School is shown here on Amwell Road around 1935. The replacement of the old one-room school was a period of new design with windows across one side of a building that contained two or four classrooms. This two-room school on Amwell Road in Hillsborough was built in 1913. After its use as a school was discontinued, it housed the Neshanic Printing Co. Today, it is home to the Somerset Valley Players. (Photograph courtesy of the Quick Family.)

# Two
# Neshanic Station of Branchburg

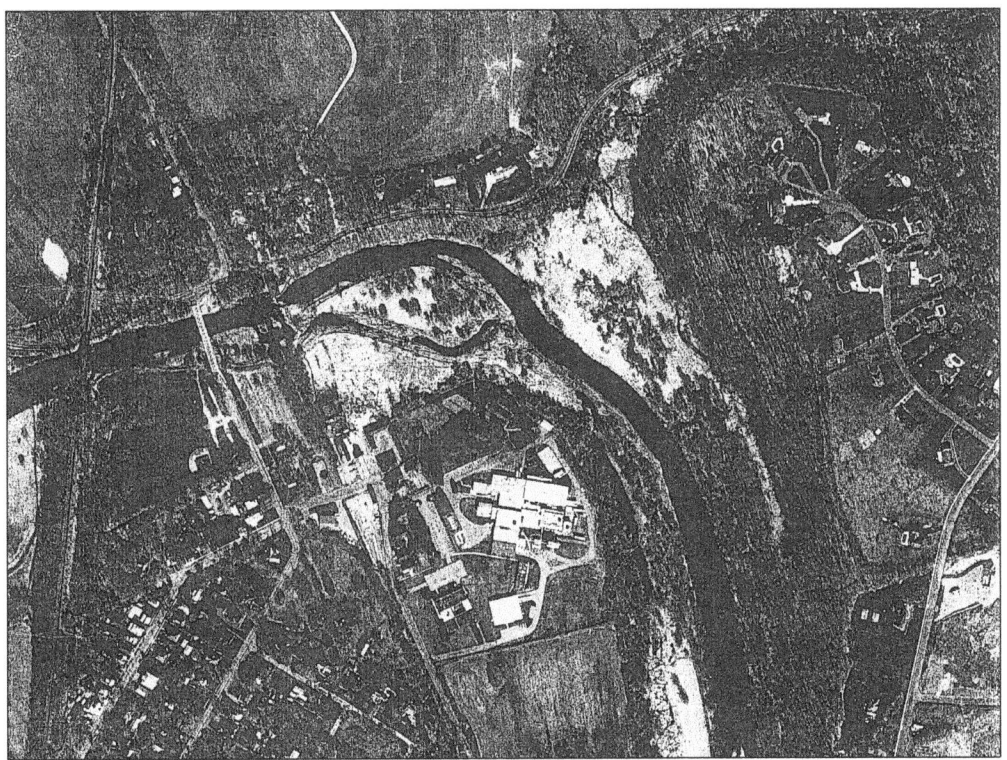

Neshanic was named by the Lenni Lenape Indians for "goose neck," as can be seen in this photograph of the south branch of the Raritan River as it winds through the Neshanic Station area. (Photograph from Somerset County 1995 Aerial Survey.)

The main street of Neshanic Station is shown here as it appeared around 1900. A full load of hay is making its way to the hay press at J.S. Amerman Co. on this tree-lined street, now known as Maple Avenue. (Photograph courtesy of Paul Kurzenberger.)

Shadowlawn (304 Maple Avenue) was built in the 1860s and is an excellent example of Italianate residential architecture. John G. Schenck, who served in the New Jersey State Senate and Assembly during the 1860s and 1870s, built the residence as a home for his family and a centerpiece for his peach farm, which encompassed most of the present-day village of Neshanic Station. He landscaped the area around the home with many trees and shrubs, the most notable being a lovely willow oak which provides a beautiful canopy shadowing much of the large front lawn. (Photograph courtesy of Neshanic Station Historical Society.)

Here, a group of people enjoy the pleasure of a peaceful mid-summer boat trip. In the past, as well as the present, the village has provided relaxation for a variety of people who have come to fish and canoe along the south branch of the Raritan River. (Photograph courtesy of M. Jane [Nevius] Brown.)

In order to provide protection for this farming community, the Neshanic Station Vigilant Society was formed in 1920, and it included many prominent citizens of the time. The members paid dues for the protection of the society. Once a theft was reported, the society was responsible for the recovery of the stolen animal or article. If not found, the society promised to reimburse the member for the theft. The society quickly went bankrupt. (Photograph courtesy of M. Jane [Nevius] Brown.)

This aerial photograph, taken in 1952, shows the complete subdivision of John Schenck's former peach farm stretching into the village of Neshanic Station. (Photograph by Walter Kostro.)

This c. 1910 photograph shows a morning carriage ride along Elm Street, looking southwest from the river. The Covert and Opie homes can be seen on the far right. (Photograph courtesy of Paul Kurzenberger.)

This view is of Neshanic Station and the surrounding farmlands in the winter of 1952-1953. The flea market grounds can be seen to the right of the Central New Jersey Railroad Station. Fairview School, the two-story brick building, which can be seen well in the upper center portion of the image, was later demolished. (Photograph taken by Walter J. Kostro, courtesy of John Vermeulen & Son.)

Homewood Acres (322 Blackpoint Road) still stands on Blackpoint Road. Here the original home can be seen as it appeared in 1887. (Photograph courtesy of Richard Hammel.)

The John Amerman residence, located at 101 Elm Street, is seen here in 1910 and was later the home of J.S.Covert. (Photograph courtesy of Paul Kurzenberger.)

Here, in the shadow of the Amerman Mill, residents can be seen harvesting the ice that formed along the south branch of the Raritan River in March 1934. (Photograph courtesy of Mary Hausch Sixt.)

Winters along the south branch of the Raritan River often challenged residents. A view from atop the Conrail freight line overpass, looking south along Pleasant Run Road, shows the heavy equipment that was needed to dig out of a major storm during the winter of 1966. (Photograph courtesy of G.W. Amerman.)

On August 28, 1971, Hurricane Doria struck the village of Neshanic Station, leaving a flood in her wake. The swollen banks of the south branch can be seen cresting. (Photograph courtesy of G.W. Amerman.)

The Brokaw Ice House, shown here, still stands behind the Neshanic Inn (now Murphy's Crocodile Inn). (Photograph courtesy of G.W. Amerman.)

When J. Bradford Opie was appointed postmaster in 1899, his general store on Woodfern Road became home for the Neshanic Station Post Office. In those days, the post office was often combined with a general store and the site of the post office moved with the appointment of a new postmaster. (Photograph courtesy of Neshanic Station Historical Society.)

In 1914, when Walter R. Huff became postmaster, the post office was moved to his general store at 211 Pearl Street, at the bend of Olive Street. (Photograph courtesy of Neshanic Station Historical Society.)

In 1917, the post office was in a separate building on the side of the general store. Note the poster urging people to buy Liberty Bonds. (Photograph courtesy of Alma Quick Deak.)

Postmistress Ruth E. Amerman is shown here in 1923. (Photograph courtesy of the Quick Family.)

In the 1950s, the post office returned to the 211 Pearl Street location after the grocery store closed. Mrs. Alma Deak, shown here with her husband, Andrew, worked in the postal service for many years. (Photograph courtesy of Alma Quick Deak.)

With the residential growth in the 1970s and 1980s, the need for a larger post office became obvious. A new post office was built on the former site of the Central Railroad of New Jersey's freight station on Main Street, across from the old passenger station and the Neshanic Methodist Church. (Photograph courtesy of G.W. Amerman.)

The Fairview School, on Fairview Drive, was one of four schools in Branchburg Township in 1880. At that time, according to Snell's History of Somerset County, the school district served by Fairview School had 74 children between five and 18 years of age. The school was supported by a total budget of $300, and the valuation of school property was listed as $1,000. Snell further recorded that Branchburg employed "one female and three male teachers at an average salary of $35 per month." (Photograph courtesy of Neshanic Station Historical Society.)

This c. 1910 photograph shows children at the Fairview Road School participating in a May pole dance. (Photograph courtesy of E. Saums.)

The one-room Fairview School was replaced by a two-story, four-room brick structure at the intersection of Marshall Street and Chester Avenue in Neshanic Station. Built in 1914, this school was also known as Fairview School. Because the state rejected the school's construction, wood floor beams with only a center hall stairway, only the two rooms on the first floor were used as classrooms. This building was phased out after Old York School was built in 1950. Even in the 1950s, when both Branchburg and Hillsborough students attended the school, it had no indoor plumbing and separate outhouses for boys and girls were used. (Photograph courtesy of Ralph Manners.)

During WW II, children from Fairview School participated in collecting salvage materials, as documented by this photograph of the "scrappers" that appeared in the *Courier News*. The children are listed as Ralph Manners (holding the flag), two sons of Mr. and Mrs. Alfred Lehman of Centerville, the two children of Mr. and Mrs. Richard Stryker of Neshanic,
Lois Amerman,
Jean Bergen, and
Harold Van Fleet.
(Photograph courtesy of A.S. Bergen, *Somerset Messenger-Gazette*.)

Fairview School class of 1940 is shown, from left to right, as follows: (front row) Joan Ogden, Ann Totten, Anna LaMarco, Betty MacQuaide, Georgianna Grenther, Gilberta Schenck, and Jean Hall; (middle row) Raymond Brokaw, Larry Totten, Ted Dilts, William Emmons, Harold Van Fleet, and Donald Henry; (back row) Eva Cromwell (teacher), Richard Krautwald, Bill Colbert, Elmer Saums, Claude Dilts, Harry Bryan, Henry Smithana, and Ed Foltin. (Photograph courtesy of Harold Van Fleet.)

Branchburg Township eighth grade graduation in 1945 was held at the Neshanic Methodist Church. Prior to 1950, the eighth grade graduation for students from all of Branchburg's schools alternated between the North Branch Reformed Church and the Neshanic Methodist Church. Graduates are shown here, from left to right, as follows: (front row) Joe Stala, Richard Melick, Kenneth Snyder, Genero Deroda, Rudolph Krautwald, Jacob Emmons, and Gerald McCray; (back row) Evelyn Breitenberger, June Stryker (Amerman), Lois Winegardner, Rosalind Fineman, Eleanor Perfumo, Frances Shimanowitz, and Doris Shimanowitz. (Photograph courtesy of June Stryker Amerman.)

Second and third grade students from Branchburg Township's Old York School are seen here visiting the J.S. Amerman Lumberyard on a class trip. Pictured here are G.W. "Bill" Amerman and the students in October 1958. (Photograph courtesy of Overbrook Studio.)

Mr. Albert F. Messig, a school bus owner-operator, is shown here in 1933, with a Fairview School class. Mr. Messig operated the first school buses from Neshanic to the local school and to Somerville High School. (Photograph courtesy of the Quick Family. Current residents Don and Jim Quick are Mr. Messig's great-grandsons.)

Shown here is the Fairview School class of 1939 with Mrs. Rosalie Severin as teacher. (Photograph courtesy of Dorothy Stryker Sipler.)

This c. 1912 photo postcard view was taken on Maple Avenue looking west showing the Quick residence with its carriage house and windmill (307 Maple Avenue). (Photo postcard courtesy of Paul Kurzenberger.)

This c. 1912 photo postcard view shows Olive Street looking west toward the Frederic Hall residence (208 Pearl Street), on the left, and the Harry Huff home (207 Pearl Street), on the right. (Photo postcard courtesy of Paul Kurzenberger.)

Mary Lavina Shurts and her husband, Garrett Stryker Shurts, were grandparents of Orville Shurts. When her husband died suddenly in 1910, the widow sold their farm in Hillsborough and had a home built on 422 Olive Street so she could be near her son, Lester Shurts. Lester Shurts had started the feed business in the old creamery on Fairview Drive in 1898 (current location of Neshanic Farm, Home & Garden Center). (Photograph courtesy of Orville Shurts.)

The residence at 422 Olive Street, built by Mary Lavina Shurts, was recently the home of our fourth justice from the area, the Honorable Robert Guterl. (Photograph courtesy of Robert Guterl.)

Dr. Richard Schlatter, one of the most prominent of the 20th-century residents of Neshanic Station, is represented here. Holder of degrees from Harvard and Oxford; recipient of multiple fellowships; and professor, provost, and vice president of Rutgers University between 1946 and 1982; Dr. Schlatter lived in the village for over 40 years. (Photograph courtesy of Heidi Schlatter Saunders.)

This image portrays Melville Wilson. Mr. Wilson purchased the Woodfern Road farm from Gordon Saunders and started Wilson Products Corp. with 10 to 12 employees in 1950. The company produced color concentrates for the plastics industry, first supplying the product for "hula hoops." Later, it served Dart Industries that produced Tupperware, as well as supplying Ford Motor Co. and Western Electric colored wire coatings. The firm grew to 120 employees and also operated a plant on Maple Avenue, opposite the Lehigh Railroad Station site. Most recently, it was operated by Dart Industries and the AKZO Corp. (See page 19 for an aerial view of the plant.) (Photograph and information courtesy of Jack Weiss.)

This portrait is of John G. Schenck. Mr. Schenck was the original owner of the Shadowlawn farm. As a railroad commissioner, he brought the south branch of the Central Railroad of New Jersey to Neshanic Station, and developed much of the commerce associated with the village. His Villa Sites, filed in 1875, became the first registered residential area in Somerset County. (See map of the subdivision on page 57.) (Portrait courtesy of John L. Schenck Jr.)

This c. 1912 Garroway studio photo postcard illustrates the Central Railroad Station in Neshanic Station. This scene shows the rebuilt J.S. Amerman Lumberyard and hay press building in background. (Courtesy of Robert Yuell.)

Louis H. Schenck was a lawyer and became a judge of the Circuit Court from 1900 to 1910. He occupied the bench at the first trial in the new Somerset County Court House, which was completed in 1909. He graduated from Rutgers University, class of 1874, and served for five years as an alumnus member of the Board of Trustees of the University, beginning in 1905. He was also president of the Branchburg Township Board of Education for 19 years. (Courtesy of John L. Schenck Jr.)

Calvin Corle, who was a state senator in the 1870s and president of the Somerset County Bank in Somerville, is shown in this photograph. He lived at the Field Crest Farm, later known as Four Pillar Farm, on South Branch Road. (See picture of farm, page 75.) (Courtesy of Robert Guterl.)

Justice Frederick W. Hall was the best known of Neshanic Station's judges. Although born without a left hand, he started school in third grade in Neshanic Station at the age of five and went on to high school at the age of ten. He graduated Phi Beta Kappa from Rutgers in 1927, and he graduated cum laude from Harvard Law School in 1931. After an exemplary legal career, he served as a justice of the New Jersey Supreme Court where he authored many noteworthy decisions, including the first *Mt. Laurel* decision. He died in 1984. (Photograph courtesy of Peter Hall.)

Justice Robert Guterl is shown here being sworn in by Judge Wilfred P. Diana, with wife, Sheryl Guterl, holding the Bible. A Neshanic resident for many years, Justice Guterl was appointed as a judge of the Superior Court of New Jersey by Governor Thomas Kean in 1989. Originally from Jersey City, he is a graduate of St. Peter's College, receiving his Juris Doctor from Rutgers Law School, in Newark, in 1964. He also did graduate work at the New York University School of Law. Justice Guterl and his family were recently the owners of the Shurts home at 422 Olive Street and among the founders of the Peanut Butter Playhouse, a children's theater group that operated in Neshanic for several years. (Photograph courtesy of the Guterl Family.)

In this c. 1900 photograph, John G. Schenck is surveying Neshanic Station from the riverside in Hillsborough Township. His Shadowlawn home is shown in the top center of the photograph. The lumberyard and coal yard, built by A.A. Cortelyou and the Central Jersey Railroad Station, are also visible. (Photograph courtesy of John L. Schenck Jr.)

This c. 1914 view down Maple Avenue shows the rock ballast from Zion Mountain, which was used below the paving done by Richards & Gaston Contracting of Somerville, New Jersey. (Photograph courtesy of L.B. Lane.)

# Three

# VILLAGE CHURCHES

Neshanic Methodist Church, built in 1907 and dedicated in 1908, cost about $6,800 to build. In 1906, local Neshanic Methodists, weary of the buggy ride to Centerville, decided to build a church and bought the lot for $350 from Senator Schenck. The first minister, John May, was given the task of raising the building funds. He met James B. Duke, the tobacco millionaire who had a home in Hillsborough Township, and Mr. Duke agreed to give $3,500 if the church could raise an equal amount. Rev. May raised $500 from the Methodist denomination. Then, while in Philadelphia for a Bible study group, he met John Wanamaker, who agreed to match with any necessary funds to have Mr. Duke pay his offer. (Photograph courtesy of the Neshanic Station Historical Society.)

This image depicts a Methodist Church Tent Meeting in 1907. Services were held here as soon as the building was started with a stone foundation. (Photograph courtesy of Robert May.)

The Methodist Church cornerstone laying ceremony is represented here in 1907. Note Senator Schenck's home, as well as the windmill tower of the adjacent Maple Street residence, in the background. (Photograph courtesy of Robert May.)

Neshanic Methodist Parsonage, with its Victorian gable front, is seen here at 315 Maple Avenue c. 1910. (Photograph courtesy of Robert Guterl.)

The interior of Neshanic Methodist Church is represented in this 1999 photograph. (Photograph by G.W. Amerman.)

Prior to the Neshanic Fire Co., the Methodist Church began the traditional clambakes. Clams were steamed on a bed of hot rocks heated by a day-long bon fire and covered with sea weed. This picture, taken in 1941, looks down Elm Street. (Photograph courtesy of the Toles Family.)

At the time of this view of the Neshanic Methodist Church in 1908, the church had been completed and services were being held, but note that the bell had not yet been placed in the belfry. (Photograph courtesy of Robert May.)

Robert May was the son of the Reverend John May, the first pastor of Neshanic Methodist Church. Bob has been a lifelong active member of this church and has been the faithful, ever-present bell ringer for nearly 50 years. (Photograph courtesy of Robert May.)

Mary Boughton touched all that knew her with her strong presence at the Neshanic Methodist Church and in the community. Drawing her strength from her Christian faith, she was always sharing her unconditional love with an encouraging word, a warm hug, or an understanding smile. Mrs. Boughton was born in September 1905, married here in 1931, and left with her husband to serve in the ministry. She taught music for many years and returned to Neshanic in 1973. Mrs. Boughton passed away in January 1999. (Photograph courtesy of Ann Boughton.)

Now over 90 years old, the Neshanic Methodist Church has a young, active membership, carrying on many of the church's traditions in the village. Every November, on Election Day, there is a traditional turkey dinner, and, during Christmas week, there is caroling at night in the streets. (Photograph courtesy of Neshanic Station Historical Society.)

Robert May, the last shepherd at the River Edge Stock Farm, is shown here in 1968. (Photograph courtesy of Robert May.)

The Circle of Seven Churches, organized in 1939, was an active group of local Protestant churches that shared in many services and related church activities, such as concerts and Lenten services. (1950 Program, sketch by Mary Kilgore; courtesy of June Stryker Amerman.)

The Neshanic Dutch Reformed Church in Hillsborough, organized in 1752, is located at the corner of Amwell Road and Main Road. This structure was completed in 1772, with stone hauled down from the Sourland Mountains by wagon. The Neshanic Reformed Church is the oldest church building in Somerset County with a continuous ministry. It is also the only public building in Somerset County not burned by the British during the Revolution. The early ministers conducted services in the Dutch language. Reverend George B. Scholten, pastor from 1926 to 1956, preached the "Historical Sermon" on October 18, 1952, celebrating 200 years. He did this using the Dutch language in his opening prayer. (Photograph courtesy of L.B. Lane.)

Since its founding in 1628, on the island known today as Manhattan, the Reformed Dutch Church has adopted as its seal an adaptation of the coat of arms of Prince William of Orange. Prince William was defender of the faith and leader of the struggle for religious freedom and national independence of the Netherlands. A beautiful walnut, hand-carved replica of the seal, dedicated in the 1980s, hangs in this church today. (Photograph courtesy of the Neshanic Reformed Church.)

This postcard picture, taken in 1952, represents the Neshanic Reformed Dutch Church. (Courtesy of the Neshanic Reformed Church.)

The First Somerset Minutemen, illustrated in this c. 1775 sketch, are forming at Neshanic Reformed Church to march off in response to General Washington's call to arms. (Sketch by John Albright, courtesy of Charles Stone.)

NESHANIC REFORMED CHURCH
Reverend Dr. Richard J. Tiggelaar, Pastor
P. O. Box 657, Neshanic Station NJ 08853-0657
(908) 369-4542

```
SOMERSET MINUTEMEN ROSTER

              MAY 1775

Captains:  John Ten Eyck, Ryner Veghte

Lieutenants:  Peter D. Vroom, John Brokaw

Second Lieutenant:  Jacobus Quick

Ensign:  Joakim Quick

Sergeants:  Minne DuBois, Andrew Van Middlesworth, Hendrick
Post, Peter Quick, Benjamin Taylor, Abraham Van Arsdale

Corporals:  Peter Brokaw, Jacobus Bergen, Thomas Coevert

Fifer:  Bergen Coevert

Privates:  Jacobus Amerman         Thomas Skillman
           Albert Amerman          Abram Stryker
           John Amerman            Jonathan Spader
           Thomas Auten            Albert Stothoff
           John Brokaw (Lieutenant when killed at Germantown)
           Abraham Brokaw          Willet Taylor
           George Brokaw           Abram Tayler
           Jacob Cook              Garret Van Arsdale
           Jacob W. Cook           John Van Dyke
           Jacobus Corshow         William Van Dyke
           Peter Ditmars           Tunis Van Middlesworth
           Nicholas DuBois         Jacobus Van Nuys
           William Griggs          Coert Van Waggoner
           Augustus Hartshough     Jacobus Voorhees
           Harmon A. Hoagland      Rynier Veghte
           Lucas Hoagland          Peter Voorhees
           Peter Hoagland          Peter Vroom
           Dirck Huff              Jacob Winter
           Abram Low               Coert Van Voorhees
           Peter Leyster
           Hugh McAllum
           Peter Perlee
```

The May 1775 Somerset Minutemen Roster is shown here. Note that many of the same families' descendants remain residents of the area today. (From *History of Troop 1776, Boy Scouts of America* by Harold DeHart.)

A NESHANIC GIRL WHO MADE GOOD — Anna Case, noted soprano, back in her home town for a concert at Dutch Reformed Church, at the organ she played twenty-one years ago. Group of local admirers includes John E. Anderson, Mrs. Issac Van Doren, Mrs. Minor Griscom, Mrs. John L. Schenck, Rev. John Hart, Mrs. George C. La Baw and Mrs. John S. Amerman.
At left, John L. Schenck, church treasurer, presents canceled check for $12, first money Miss Case ever receivd for singing. In background are Miss Case's mother, Mrs. Jeannette Case, and her first music teacher, Miss Katherine Updycke.
(Staff Photos, H. C. Dorer.)

Anna Case, noted soprano from South Branch, is shown here playing the Reformed Church organ at a recital in 1930. The organ was one of many placed in area churches by the Andrew Carnegie Foundation. (Photograph from the Newark Sunday Call, courtesy of June Stryker Amerman.)

A new organ, placed in the Neshanic Reformed Church, was dedicated to Alida Kip Totten on May 23, 1982, and renamed as the "Harry S. and Alida K. Totten Memorial Organ" in 1984. (Photograph courtesy of the Neshanic Reformed Church.)

This small portrait is of Alida Kip Totten, 1901–1980. (Photograph courtesy of the Neshanic Reformed Church.)

This interior view of Neshanic Reformed Church shows the pulpit area, including the WW II servicemen's star flag. Each star represented a member in the armed forces. The stained-glass windows were replaced with new windows in 1963. (Photograph courtesy of the Neshanic Reformed Church.)

Mabel Stryker Neary is shown here on her way to church on Amwell Road, at the corner of Wertsville Road, around 1910. (Photograph courtesy of G.W. Amerman.)

Neshanic Reformed Church parking lot is shown here at the time of the 175th Anniversary on October 26, 1927. (Photograph courtesy of the Neshanic Reformed Church.)

Pictured here is Neshanic Reformed Church's fourth parsonage at 722 Amwell Road, opposite the church parking area. It was the residence of five pastors. The car shown is that of Reverend Dr. John Hart in 1924. (Photograph courtesy of L.B. Lane.)

This is Brookside Hall, Neshanic Reformed Church Sunday school, shown in the mid-1950s. This view shows how the church enlarged the original one-room school, whose belfry is still showing and contains the bell. (Photograph courtesy of Stanley Wood.)

This *c.* 1900 postcard view of the Neshanic Reformed Church shows Dr. Andersen's home to the left and the original one-room school on the right. (Photograph courtesy of L.B. Lane.)

A Tom Thumb wedding, performed by Sunday school students in October 1950, is shown here shortly after Brookside Hall auditorium was enlarged. The participants were as follows: Marjorie Shepherd, bride; George Wallace, groom; David Totten, minister. (Towne Studio Photograph, courtesy of Rev. George Scholten.)

# Four

# RAILROADS

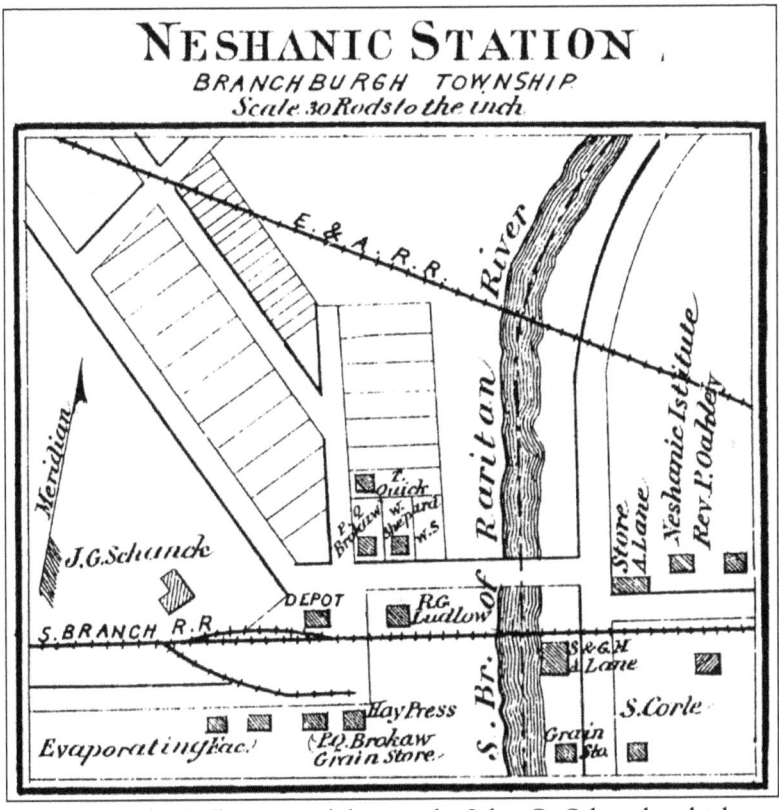

This 1875 map shows the Villa Sites subdivision by John G. Schenck, which was Somerset County's first registered subdivision. By the mid-19th century, the railroads were already a major presence in Neshanic Station, with the Easton and Amboy Railroad (later the Lehigh Valley Railroad) on the east side of the village and the South Branch Railroad (later the Central Railroad of New Jersey) on the west.

This freight station, now long gone, served the Central Railroad of New Jersey near the passenger station. It was one of several stations that served the immediate area of Neshanic Station. It was here, around the turn of the century, that wagons of peaches were unloaded for shipment to New York City. (Photograph courtesy of Walt Kostro.)

This is the only picture known to exist of the original bridge over the south branch of the Raritan River, which was built for the Easton and Amboy Railroad and later replaced. Trainloads of peaches, such as the one pictured here, were shipped regularly to New York from Neshanic Station. (Photograph courtesy of the Neshanic Station Historical Society.)

This passenger station on the Lehigh Railroad tracks stood next to a local creamery, both of which are now gone. They stood across the tracks from the Shurts feed store, now the Neshanic Farm, Home, and Garden Store (on Fairview Drive). Another Lehigh Station was located less than a mile away, across the river, on the Hillsborough side. (Photo postcard courtesy of Robert Yuell.)

This postcard shows the center of the village in 1906, before the fire that destroyed a number of the buildings shown here. The grassy parcel of property in the foreground is now the site of the post office. (Photo postcard courtesy of Robert Yuell.)

By the time of this picture, trees had grown along the riverbank. The railroad cars shown here were noticeably larger than those shown in an earlier picture, but coal was still king. (Photograph courtesy of Joan Levering.)

This *c.* 1908 postcard of the Central Railroad of New Jersey at Neshanic Station shows the creamery (with cupola), where the 1910 fire started; the J.S. Amerman Co. hay press; and rail cars under the overhang. (Photo postcard courtesy of Robert Yuell.)

Camelback engines like the ones shown above, with the engineer's cab straddling the engine, were a common sight in Neshanic Station from the turn of the century into the 1940s. (Photo postcard courtesy of Robert Yuell.)

Train wrecks, like this one in the 1950s, were not common in the area of Neshanic Station. The tracks of both railroads were very straight approaching the village, but equipment failures and operator error took a toll. (Photograph courtesy of the Toles family.)

The approaching demise of the Central Railroad of New Jersey is evident from this 1952 photograph. The station is in obvious disrepair and the camelback engine is probably over 40 years old, but until 1953, you could still commute from Neshanic Station to New York (or to Somerville or Flemington!). (Photograph courtesy of Walt Kostro.)

Within a year of the end of passenger service (and a few years before the end of freight service), grass had started to take over the right of way. The mill and the telegraph wires can be seen in the background. Today, the telegraph wires are gone, and the mill has now become a residence after restoration. (Photograph courtesy of Walt Kostro.)

This scene shows passengers boarding at Neshanic Station for the last run to Flemington on April 24, 1953. (Photograph by Homer R. Hill.)

The Hunterdon County Agriculture Commission annual excursion to West Point and Bear Mountain, via Circle Line Ferry boats, is shown here pulled by engine number 1286 at Neshanic Station. These were the longest passenger trains seen on the South Branch Line with two runs of 10 to 12 cars each. (Photograph courtesy of Somerset County Historical Society.)

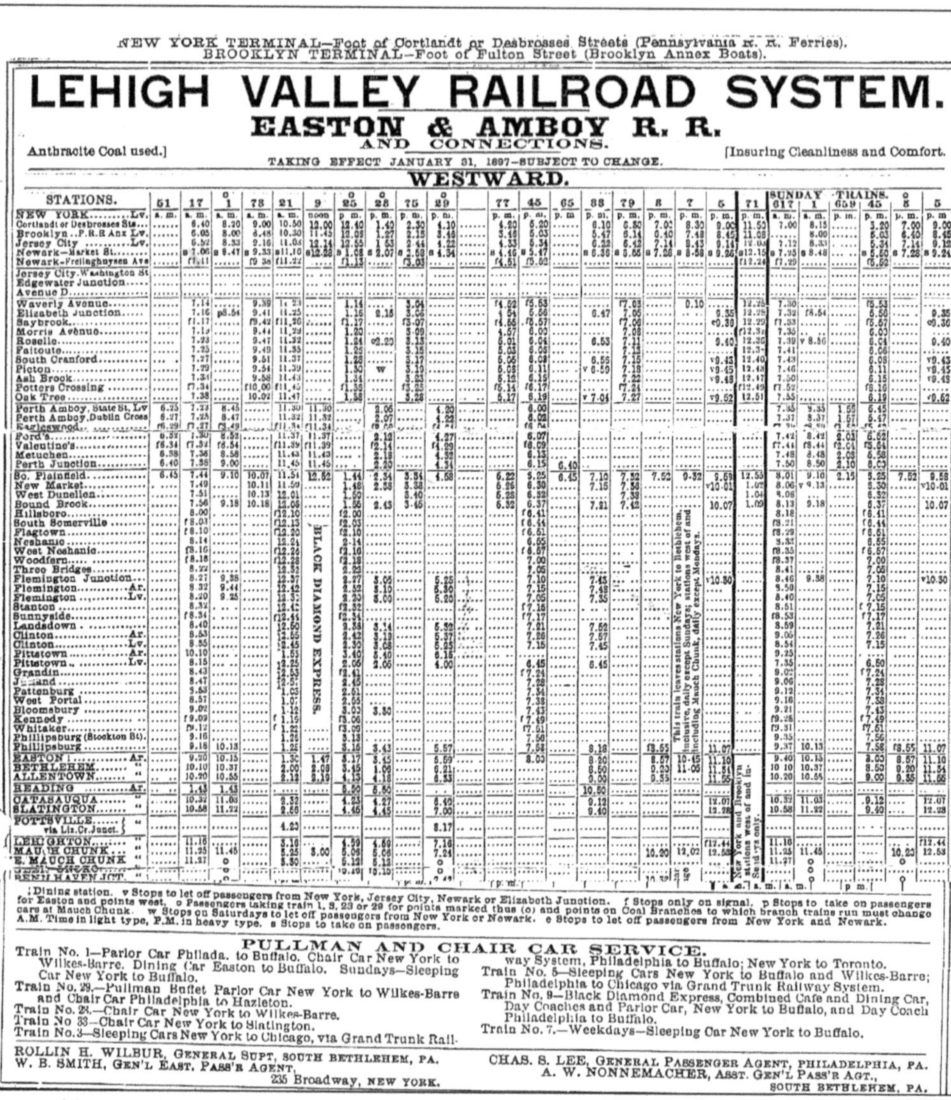

Pictured here is the 1897 Easton and Amboy Railroad schedule of the Lehigh Valley Railroad System, showing the two Neshanic stations. (Courtesy of Robert Yuell.)

# Five
# NESHANIC VOLUNTEER FIRE COMPANY

The need for a local fire company became evident in 1910, when a major blaze destroyed the eastern edge of the village. The fire started in a creamery by the Central Jersey Railroad. The boiler that exploded is by the large tree on the left of the picture. Two rail cars were consumed by the blaze at the J.S. Amerman hay press building. The lumberyard, Holcombe's Hotel, and the Schenck farm (to the far rear) were all destroyed. (Photograph courtesy of G.W. Amerman.)

Over the two days following the fire, the creamery building, shown here ablaze on September 28, 1910, attracted hundreds of people who flocked to see the devastation. (Photo postcard courtesy of Robert Yuell.)

This postcard is dated 1907 and depicts the creamery by the Central Jersey Railroad Station during its active days. (Photo postcard courtesy of Robert Yuell.)

Somerville Engine Co. No. 1 was brought by special flatcar train to Neshanic to help quell the embers of the coal yard fire over the two days after the fire began. This engine returned to Neshanic in the early 1990s during an antique fire equipment muster sponsored in Neshanic. (Photograph by Charles F. Karbowski, courtesy of Somerville Firemen's Museum.)

The first firehouse, a 20-by-30-foot garage, was built in 1928. Most of the funds were raised by the Ladies Auxiliary, chaired by Mrs. J.S. Covert. Many events were held, including suppers and auctions, and much labor was volunteered during the construction of the firehouse. (Photograph courtesy of Neshanic Volunteer Fire Co.)

In 1933, an auditorium and kitchen were added to the firehouse. These provided the company space to hold other fund-raising events, as well as suppers and card parties. During the 1930s, the fire company also held a week-long carnival near the Fairview School by Marshall Street. This photograph shows the Blawenburg Band playing during the dedication ceremonies. (Photograph courtesy of Neshanic Volunteer Fire Co.)

A third addition, started in 1949 and completed in 1951, housed the original Pirsch pumper and the 1950 Studebaker utility pumper. (Photograph courtesy of Neshanic Volunteer Fire Co.)

The Neshanic Volunteer Fire Co. and its 1929 Pirsch pumper are shown here in the Raritan Basilone Day Parade in 1988. The pumper, with the first Hahn International pumper, was retired in 1963. Shown here are Len Brown and Tom Van Glahn (driving). (Photograph by Doug Merrill.)

The 1951 Neshanic Volunteer Fire Co. members, showing their first uniforms, are ready for the Lions Club Memorial Day Parade and service. Fire company members shown here, from left to right, are as follows: Simon Nevius, John R. Gaddis, Varian Quick Jr., Ralph Ricker, Irving Covert, Peter Emery, Larry Lee, Harold Van Glahn, Joseph Berger, Irving Connett, George Covert, Bill Amerman, John O'Brien Jr., Max Gwin, Andrew Deak, Robert Strong, Clark Scully, Harold O'Brien, and Henry Schuler. (Photograph courtesy of Neshanic Volunteer Fire Co.)

The 1982 Firemen's Parade is shown here starting down Maple Avenue, from the firehouse, with Chief Jack Knower leading the crew. (Photograph courtesy of Alma Quick Deak.)

The 1950 Studebaker pumper is shown here passing in review under a cable television camera boom truck on Maple Avenue in 1978. Retired in 1968, this pumper came out of storage and was loaned to Hillsborough Fire Co. No. 2 in 1972, while one of the company's pumpers was being repaired. It was the last time the truck was in service. (Photograph courtesy of G.W. Amerman.)

Neshanic's Studebaker, with its 500-gallon-per-minute, front-mounted pump, became much traveled. Since it was unique as a Studebaker firetruck, it was included in many antique firetruck musters. Here the firetruck is shown in 1998, in England, where it serves in complete array (as part of the décor) in a deep pan pizza restaurant near Manchester, in the Bury-Lancaster Mall. (Photograph courtesy of Tom Van Glahn.)

John O'Brien Jr. and Max Gwin pose by the Hunnewell pumper, restored by Mr. O'Brien for the Neshanic Volunteer Fire Company. This hand-drawn pumper has won many awards in parades and was still demonstrated in use during the 1990 antique equipment muster at the Firemen's Field. It still pumps with eight healthy men pulling the bars. (Photograph by Bob Young, courtesy of the Hillsborough Beacon.)

In 1958, Orville Shurts donated a large parcel of land on Maple Avenue to the Neshanic Volunteer Fire Company, and the new fire headquarters is located here. From 1958 to 1960, the fire company constructed a fire pond with a gravity hydrant system in the village. This picture shows the start of the excavation by Vollers Construction Co., from left to right, as follows: (front row) Branchburg Mayor Walter O'Brien, George Covert, Bill Amerman, and George Fenwick; (back row) Harold Van Glahn, Dave Bullock, Irving Covert, and Chris McTameny. (Photograph by Harvey Patterson, courtesy of Neshanic Volunteer Fire Company.)

Neshanic Firemen's popular clambakes were held at various locations through the 1960s. This view, in the late 1950s, shows a clambake in the Firemen's Field across from the Neshanic Flea Market on Elm Street. The large tent was owned by the Neshanic Reformed Church and used for Harvest Home Suppers. (Photograph courtesy of the Toles family.)

Fire Chief John O'Brien is shown here keeping some of the ladies supplied with clams and birch beer. The ladies shown here, from left to right, are as follows: June Amerman, Ruth Quick, Ruth Messig, and Edith Wargo. (Photograph by G.W. Amerman.)

The 1998 Memorial Day celebration, at current headquarters, is shown here. Some of the participants are, from left to right, as follows: (first row) Len Brown, Thomas Van Glahn, Jim Covert, Darcy Marshall, Max Gwin, Joseph Cangelosi, and Thomas Bittle; (second row) Larry Booker, Emilio Suarez, John Hance, Chris Suarez, Dan Clerico, John Lazorchak, Bill Iden, Charles Davis, George Murphy, and Eric Jensen; (third row) Keith Covert, John Andreychak, Richard Bullock, David Gwin, Andy Preston, and Richard Malko. (Photograph courtesy of Neshanic Volunteer Fire Co.)

The weekend before Christmas, Santa appears in all of the Branchburg Township streets included in the area served by the Neshanic Volunteer Fire Company. Here, youngsters anxiously await his coming with candy canes, as he is preceded by the newest truck in the fleet. (Photograph by G.W. Amerman.)

Neshanic Volunteer Fire Company's fleet of seven trucks is shown here in January 1999, in front of the Maple Avenue fire headquarters. This building was dedicated in 1977, by Congresswoman Millicent Fenwick. (Photograph by G.W. Amerman.)

# Six
# AGRICULTURE

Pilfour Dairy Farm (2367 South Branch Road) is pictured here in 1947. Also known as Four Pillar Farm, it was operated by B.J. Goldsmith. Built in 1837 by Peter T. Beekman, it was owned in 1855 by Calvin Corle, who served as a New Jersey state senator in the 1870s. (Photograph courtesy of G.W. Amerman.)

The Housel Farm, at 2352 South Branch Road, is a typical small dairy farm with a hay storage barn, poultry house, windmill, and machine shed. This farm is one of two very similar early farms in this area. Each had the same house plan, and the barns were built similarly on a hillside facing the southeast. (See photograph of Arch S. Amerman Farm.) (Photograph courtesy of G.W. Amerman.)

The Arch S. Amerman Farm is situated in Hillsborough, at 1140 River Road. (See description of the Housel Farm.) Mr. Amerman also owned the A.S.A. Feed Mill. (Photograph courtesy of Paul Kurzenberger.)

River Edge Stock Farm, seen here, is located on South Branch River Road in Neshanic and was in the Huff family for many generations. The farm was originally the property of Tunis Huff, who owned about 500 acres of land in Neshanic. His daughter Sarah married John G. Schenck, who laid out the town of Neshanic Station. Tunis's son Abram T. Huff became the owner of River Edge Farm. In 1903, the farm was purchased by John V. Huff. After his death in 1914, his widow and sons continued to operate the farm. In 1938, the farm had 40 Guernsey milk cows and a flock of 100 Cheviot sheep imported from England. (Photograph courtesy of G.W. Amerman.)

Anna Griscom, another descendant of the Huffs, is pictured here at the age of 91 in a December 1969 sleigh ride at the River Edge Farm. Mrs. Griscom was the mother of Mary Boughton of Neshanic Station. (Photograph courtesy of E. Saums.)

Halliday McCall's Opie Road farm is depicted here. Mr. McCall built the large dairy barn shown here after a fire destroyed earlier barns. The present owner is a trainer for the U.S. Olympic Equestrian team, and the barn and fields are used for horses. This is typical of the many changes taking place in agriculture in the area. (Photograph courtesy of G.W. Amerman.)

The Hastings Farm on Zion Road shows a typical Canadian double silo dairy barn built just prior to the start of the 20th century. Mr. Hastings had moved here from Richford, Vermont, a prominent French-Canadian dairy farm area. The middle barn was built in the 1950s by Berton J. Todd to house more dairy cows. The barn on the left was built by Mr. Hastings for hay storage, horse stalls, and machinery storage. (Photograph courtesy of G.W. Amerman.)

John Vermeulen, founder of John Vermeulen & Son Wholesale Nurserymen, emigrated from Holland and began his business in 1921, in Westbury, New York, before moving to Neshanic in 1947. (Photograph courtesy of J. Peter Vermeulen.)

Three generations of the Vermeulen family have been involved in the nursery business in Neshanic. Pictured are John Vermeulen's son J. Peter and his grandchildren Nancy and Jeff. (Photograph courtesy of G.W. Amerman.)

Simon Nevius and son David show off a John Deere 730 Diesel from J.S. Covert & Sons, in this c. 1958 photograph. (Photograph courtesy of M. Jane [Nevius] Brown.)

Hill Top Farm, off Pleasant Run Road, is shown in this c. 1903 photograph with its new owner Isaac Livingston Kip (seated on stump). (Photograph courtesy of Francis Totten.)

Isaac Livingston Kip (at 63 years of age) is pictured in May 1934, with grandson Francis Totten, aged two and a half years. The buckskin team of Bucky and Charlie were born and raised in the west, shipped east in 1932, and purchased by Mr. Kip. Note the brand on the left rump of Charlie. (Photograph courtesy of Francis Totten.)

A wood-burning steam engine is shown here running a thresher at the Sebring Farm at 721 Amwell Road, *c.* 1890. (Photograph courtesy of L.B. Lane.)

This c. 1890 image portrays poultry at large on the Sebring Farm (721 Amwell Road). Note the grinding wheel stone by the large tree. This photograph also affords a great view of an adjustable roof hay barrack, cornstalk thatch, and corncrib attached to the end of the barn. (Photograph courtesy of L.B. Lane.)

This pastoral scene of Holstein dairy cows at the Kanach Farm on South Branch Road has almost disappeared from the area. (Photograph by G.W. Amerman.)

# Seven
# Commerce and Industry

The John C. Lane Store stood at the corner of Amwell and River Roads, in Neshanic, next to Dr. Andersen's home. The store building burned on May 18, 1918. Today, the foundation is still visible between the Bassuk home and the Lane corner home. This photograph dates to 1900. (Photograph courtesy of L.B. Lane.)

This c. 1904 photograph taken by Laura Lane shows Mr. R.V. Gulick, an early local butcher, with his retail delivery wagon at the corner near J.C. Lane's store and the Neshanic Reformed Church. (Photograph courtesy of L.B. Lane.)

The R.V. Gulick local butcher shop was located at 405 Olive Street, in Neshanic Station, in the same building that housed the post office during the 1940s (when Mr. Willis Hoagland and Mrs. Edna McTameny were postmasters). (Photograph courtesy of L.B. Lane.)

This c. 1904 photograph shows the A.S. Amerman Mill (at 1127 River Road) that burned in 1926, during a snowstorm. (Photograph courtesy of Neshanic Station Historical Society.)

The rebuilt A.S. Amerman Mill, located in the Neshanic Historical District in Hillsborough, is shown here in 1929. The mill was rebuilt with four rather than five floors, as was the case in the original mill. The dam and forebay upstream fed the undershot water-powered mill machinery. (Photograph courtesy of George Longacre.)

This flour bag shows the brand manufactured by the Neshanic Mill. (Photograph courtesy of G.W. Amerman.)

This image presents a present-day view of the Neshanic Mill (1127 River Road), taken in September 1998. It is now a beautifully restored residence. (Photograph courtesy of G.W. Amerman.)

Andrew Lane's Mill and Store, with residence attached, was located at the River Road end of Mill Lane, just opposite the A.S. Amerman Mill. This photo postcard, taken in 1904, shows the Lehigh Valley Railroad Station at the top of the hill. At that time, there were two stations: this station and another called West Neshanic Station (located by the Shurts Feed mill on Fairview Drive). (Photograph courtesy of the Neshanic Station Historical Society.)

W.O. Ackerman, a Rural Free Delivery (RFD) mailman, is shown by the J. Bradford Opie General Store and Post Office with his horse and buggy in August 1909. (Photo postcard courtesy of Robert Yuell.)

This view, from C.R.R. freight house, shows the Opie store with meat market (in middle) and Knights of Pythias Lodge (on right). Note the message card, postmarked April 13, 1908. (Photo postcard courtesy of Robert Yuell.)

The J. Bradford Opie store, which he operated for 50 years, was continued by his cousin, V.W. Opie. Clark Scully operated a general store at this location for a few more years. Then Otho Saums and son Elmer Saums sold electrical appliances here while operating as Neshanic Electric Co. The building has now been restored as a residence. (Photograph courtesy of Walt Kostro.)

The Shurts Brothers' original building (101 Fairview Drive), which is still operating as Neshanic Station Farm and Garden, is owned by Walter Maze (pictured here by the door). This building was originally a cheese factory with a residence on the second floor. (Photograph by G.W. Amerman, 1998.)

Orville Shurts (at the age of 95) is shown in this October 1998 photograph by the scalehouse and office, which he operated after the death of his father, Lester, and uncle, Andrew Shurts. Orville Shurts still stops in to check on business with Walter Maze. (Photograph by G.W. Amerman, 1998.)

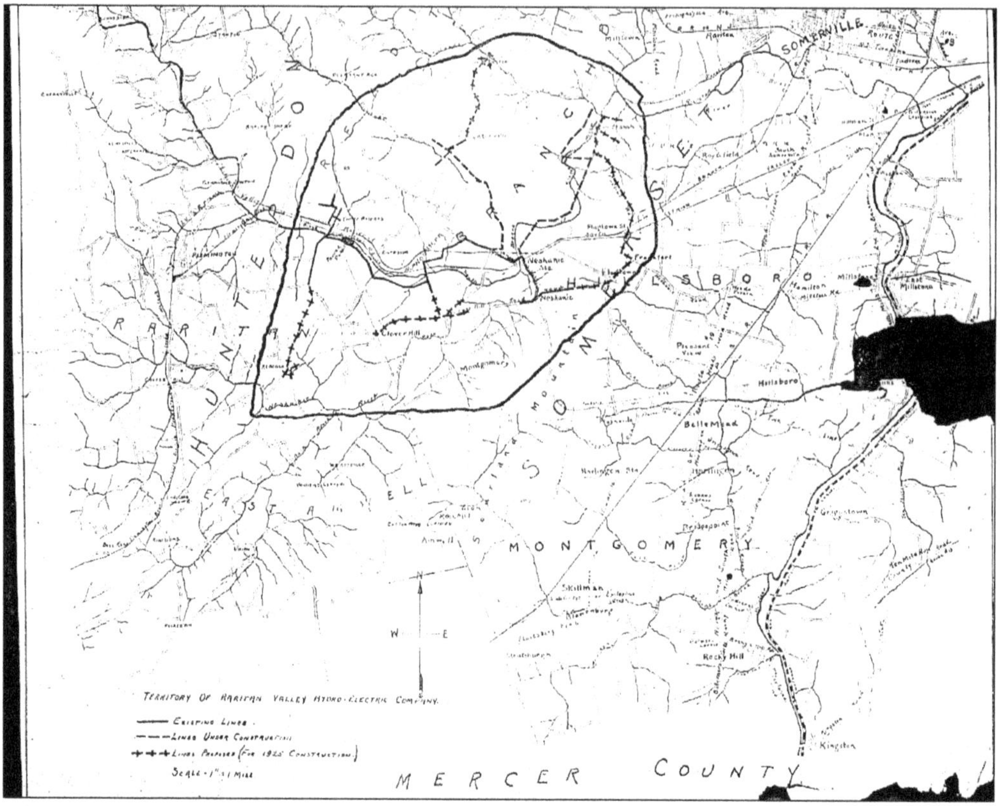

This is a map of the Raritan Valley Hydroelectric Co. started in 1922. Powered at the Higginsville Mill (below Three Bridges), the Raritan Valley Hydroelectric Co. supplied the first electricity to the villages of Neshanic and Neshanic Station with an undershot waterwheel. Founded by John S. Amerman, Harry V. Hoff, and Frank Van Syckle, the company was later incorporated into the NJ Power & Light Co. (Courtesy of Neshanic Station Historical Society.)

Hoff's Electrical Service at 421 Olive Street was started in 1948, by David F. Hoff, and is now celebrating 50 years in commercial and residential wiring service. The electric service began in one of D.C. R. Hoff's poultry houses. Starting with the firm in 1973, Douglas C. Hoff III is now the president. Here he proudly sits in his office with his great-grandfather Harry Barker's original barbershop chair as décor. (Photograph by G.W. Amerman, 1999.)

Michael Hausch, a blacksmith, is shown in this c. 1920 photograph at work by his forge. His shop was located on Mill Lane, just above Andrew Lane's Mill and Store. (Photograph courtesy of Mary Hausch Sixt.)

This is one of Mr. Hausch's statements, for the Shurts Brothers' Mill, showing prices for horseshoes, chain repair, etc. over several months in 1920. (Courtesy of Orville Shurts.)

This is a photograph of the blacksmith shop operated by Mike Hausch, which shows a wood stave, waterwagon, as well as various buggies and wagons with wheels awaiting iron work at his Mill Lane forge. (Photograph courtesy of Mary Hausch Sixt.)

**QUALITY CHICKS DESERVE QUALITY TRANSPORTATION**

A large per cent of Hoff's Vitality-Quality chicks are sold nearer home each season. This is, perhaps because they are best known at home and I can come in personal contact with the purchaser. With this 1927 Model Master Six Buick I deliver, with all the comforts of a Pullman car, 4000 or more chicks within a radius of 30 miles. Smaller orders are delivered in proportion to the number of chicks ordered. All Parcel Post shipments are delivered direct from my hatching cellars to mail trains without being exposed to the elements of the weather, the Postmaster affixing and cancelling the stamps at my hatching plant.

Shown here is an advertisement for the Hoff chick delivery service. This 1927 Buick Master Six was ordered by a funeral director who was unable to take delivery, so Mr. Hoff bought a deluxe delivery van. (Photograph courtesy of Douglas Hoff III.)

D.C. R. Hoff, one of America's pioneer chick producers, established his business in 1888. This photograph dates back to 1925. (Photograph courtesy of Virginia Hoff.)

Photographic reproduction of advertisement as it appeared in the May 18, 1912 issue of the Rural New-Yorker, 36 years ago. That issue carried 45 poultry advertisements. To the best of my knowledge I am the only one remaining in the poultry business today.

**D. C. R. HOFF**

NESHANIC                 NEW JERSEY

TELEPHONE NESHANIC 4-6511

**HOFF'S DAY OLD CHICKS**
SINGLE COMB WHITE LEGHORNS
MATURE QUICKLY        LAY EARLY
BUY BABY CHICKS AND AVOID WORRY AND LOSS

I have my own pens of breeding stock, carefully bred for large egg production as well as exhibition purposes. For twenty years I have given special attention to a Strain that develops and matures early so as to come into laying in the fewest possible number of days. That is why my May and June hatched chicks do so well. This year they are especially desirable because of the late Spring, which has hindered so many who depend on hens and small incubators.

Read what one of my customers writes of my baby chicks.

The chicks that I bought of you last Spring are giving close to 70% egg production this month, December, when "eggs are eggs." They seem to take great delight in laying.
R. V. Rex, Uniontown, Pa.

We guarantee to fill all orders with properly hatched, vigorous chicks, that will improve your flock, or start you right in the poultry business. All chicks are hatched in a 6,000 egg mammoth and 15 sand tray Prairie State incubators with perfectly sanitary surroundings, and receive the benefit of my twenty-three years' experience in artificial incubation.

HATCHING EGGS FOR SALE. I have for sale S. C. White Leghorn eggs of highest fertility, $1.50 per 15; $6.00 per 100.

I would like to send you my illustrated booklet and low prices on "vitality" Chicks of QUALITY. Write me and you will not be disappointed.

D. C. R. HOFF, Lock Box 115, NESHANIC STATION, N. J.

Shown here is one of Hoff's day-old chick advertisements, dated May 1912. (Courtesy of Virginia Hoff.)

This view shows part of the interior of the incubator cellar located beneath D.C. R. Hoff's home at 420 Olive Street in Neshanic Station. Two incubators had a capacity of over 30,000 eggs. (Photograph courtesy of Douglas Hoff III.)

This c. 1914 photograph captures the Metz Car Agency operated by George Quick at 416 Olive Street in Neshanic Station. This same building housed D.C. R. Hoff Poultry, the original Hoff's Electrical Service, a bakery, and a firetruck. Today, a barber shop and a residence are located in the building. (Photograph courtesy of Neshanic Station Historical Society.)

Maude Quick is shown here serving a customer in her general store at 695 Amwell Road in Neshanic, near the two-room school. When Maude started an ice cream and candy store in her home, it became so successful that her husband gave up his business, Metz Garage. They built a new store next door to their home and operated a very successful butcher shop and general store until 1960. (Photograph courtesy of Arthur Saunders.)

The former Quick's General Store, located at 695 Amwell Road, later became the home of Hillsborough Lawn and Garden Center shown here, operated by L.B. Lane and family. This photograph was taken c. 1970. (Photograph courtesy of L.B. Lane.)

Holcombe's Hotel is shown here after it was rebuilt, following the 1910 fire. The original was built in 1875 after the coming of the Central Railroad of New Jersey. The sign on the rear building shows the location of Harry Barker's barbershop and the poolroom. Note the separate ladies and gents entrances to the hotel. (Photograph courtesy of Neshanic Station Historical Society.)

Neshanic Inn, formerly Holcombe's Hotel, was owned in 1930 by A.F. Messig, who sold Gulf gasoline and kerosene at the Riverside Garage. The hotel housed a tavern through the door on the left, a meat market in the center, and a Breyer's Ice Cream shop through the door on the right. The adjacent business, J.S. Amerman Building Material, is also shown. (Photograph courtesy of the Quick Family.)

Shown here is an advertisement for Riverside Garage. (Courtesy of the Quick Family.)

# RIVERSIDE GARAGE
## Neshanic Station, N. J.

Automobile Tires, Tubes, and Accessories
Oils, Greases, Etc.

## GULF GAS.   GULF KEROSENE.

Recharging of all makes of Batteries and the best Batteries for sale.

Don't neglect your Tires as Riverside Garage has Free Air.

Tires cost money, Air costs nothing.

Tractor Oil and all other Oils
at special prices in 5 gallon lots or over.

Repairing of all kinds promptly done.

Snell's *History* and some other articles refer to a coffin factory located in Neshanic Station. This c. 1900 photograph is the only known picture of the factory, showing it near the driveway entry to the Totten farm, located on Otto Road. (Photograph courtesy of Frank Totten.)

J.S. Covert's Garage building on Pearl Street is shown here in 1923 with Mr. Covert in the foreground. (Photograph courtesy of Jim Covert.)

J. Staats Covert and Jeanette Covert are shown here celebrating their 60th wedding anniversary in 1970. Mr. and Mrs. Covert were active in shaping the community. J.S. Covert & Sons was the largest John Deere equipment dealer in New Jersey from 1928 to 1987, and also sold Studebaker cars and trucks from 1937 to 1965. Mrs. Covert started the Bright Buttons 4-H Club in the 1920s. Mr. and Mrs. Covert were instrumental in fund-raising for the creation of the fire company and were charter members. (Photograph courtesy of the Covert Family.)

The enlarged J.S. Covert & Sons business is shown here in 1947, with the J.S. Amerman Co., new Studebaker coal truck. (Photograph by A. Schenck Bergen, unpublished work, courtesy of Olivia Cutler.)

Cars, Inc., owned by Glenn D. Cecchine, took over the former J.S. Covert & Sons location and deals in antique automobiles and parts, specializing in Buick cars. The business started in 1974, and it moved to Neshanic in 1987. (Photograph courtesy of Glenn Cecchine.)

The A. Schenck Bergen home and business are shown here in 1930, at 606 Marshall Street in Neshanic Station. Mr. Bergen sold Allis Chalmers tractors and machinery, as well as Surge milking machines. This is the present location of Don's Service Center. (Photograph by A. Schenck Bergen, unpublished work, courtesy of Olivia Cutler.)

A.S. Bergen's Ford truck is shown here with a new, early model Allis Chalmers combine. (Photograph by A. Schenck Bergen, unpublished work, courtesy of Olivia Cutler.)

A.S. Bergen employees are shown in the early 1930s, from left to right, as follows: (front row) Perry Packer, William E. Favier, John M. Agans Jr., and A.S. Bergen; (back row) an unknown person and Herbert Ireland. Somerset County Road Department barn is also shown here, in right rear. (Photograph by A. Schenck Bergen, unpublished work, courtesy of Olivia Cutler.)

Francis Hultz's truck is shown in this 1930s photograph on Woodfern Road, near the former Gerola Brothers bakery, which was then used as his truck garage. Francis and Lewis Hultz hauled hay and straw from this area to Long Island, as well as delivering coal from Pennsylvania mines to local users. (Photograph by A. Schenck Bergen, unpublished work, courtesy of Olivia Cutler.)

The J.S. Amerman Co. Lumber, Coal, and Feed business is seen here on Woodfern Road, opposite the Central Railroad Station. This photo postcard from 1908 shows the creamery building (with cupola) where the 1910 fire originated. (Photograph courtesy of Robert Yuell.)

# JOHN S. AMERMAN

### Candidate for

### Member of Assembly

Paid for by John S. Amerman Campaign Manager

John S. Amerman, candidate for the New Jersey Assembly, was proprietor of the lumberyard from 1906 to 1931. He was a member of the New Jersey Assembly from 1917 to 1919. (Photograph courtesy of J.S. Amerman Co. Collection.)

A snow storm was captured in this image on March 19, 1956. George W. Amerman Sr., second generation owner of J.S. Amerman Co., stands in the doorway on what appears to be a very slow business day. (Photograph courtesy of J.S. Amerman Co. Collection.)

The 50th anniversary of J.S. Amerman Co. (100 Woodfern Road) took place in 1956. Employees, shown here, are G.W. Amerman Jr., Alan Melick, Mae Ten Eyck, President G.W. Amerman Sr., William B. Spratt, Fred Boyd, and Ted Miller. (Photograph courtesy of J.S. Amerman Co. Collection.)

Pictured here is Varian V.C. Quick Sr. Ice Cream and Stationery Store at 409 Olive Street, Neshanic Station, c. 1934. The store at this location was operated by several owners and is now a residence. (Photograph courtesy of Alma Quick Deak.)

Winfield Case and his wife, Lillie, operated the store at the same Olive Street location for 17 years. (Photo postcard courtesy of Gwen Jamele.)

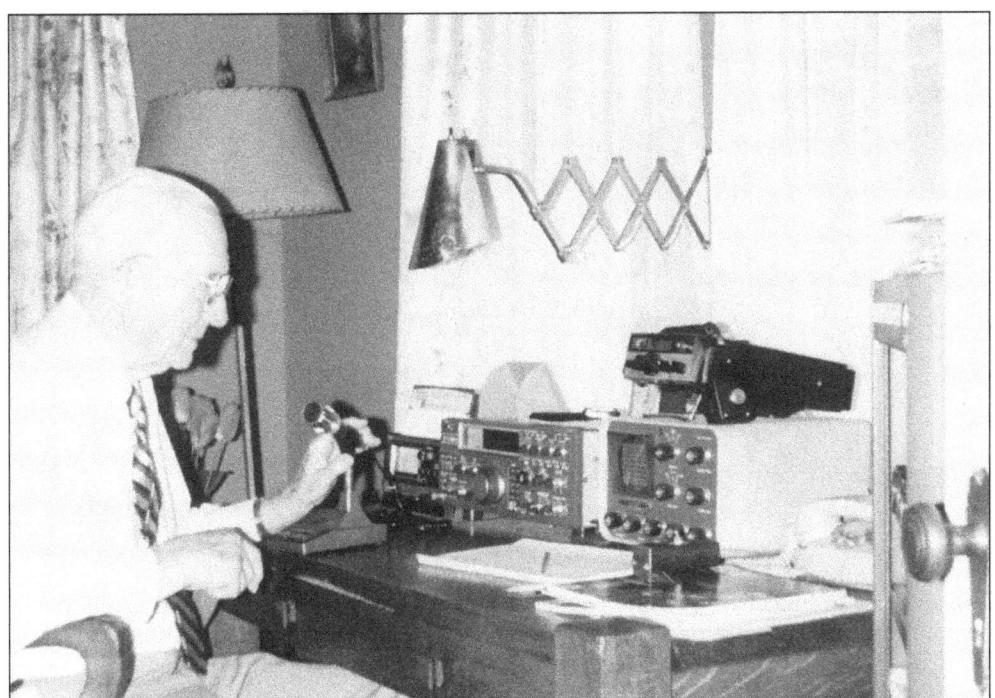

Horace Brokaw started business in 1922, building wireless radio sets for friends. He is seen here in 1972, talking on his Ham radio, celebrating 50 years in business. Mr. Brokaw served as president of the Branchburg Board of Education for 18 years. (Photograph courtesy of H.R. Brokaw.)

An H.R. Brokaw Co. service truck is shown here in front of a new showroom and shop at 688 Case Road, which was used from 1962 until he retired in 1984. (Photograph courtesy of H.R. Brokaw.)

The wide use of Studebakers in the Neshanic area, sold by J.S. Covert & Sons, is illustrated here. A farmer is transporting a heifer from one farm to another on a mid-1930s truck, and a 1950 Studebaker car is waiting to join him. (Photograph courtesy of the Toles family.)

The Tuscarora Pennsylvania Pipeline crew is shown here at the Neshanic Hotel on Amwell Road in the 1920s. They stayed at the hotel while laying the oil pipeline along the Amwell Valley from Pennsylvania to Linden, New Jersey. (Photograph courtesy of L.B. Lane.)

This is an aerial view of the Williams Corp. Transco Gas Line, along South Branch Road, in Branchburg Township. This pipeline compression station entered the area in the early 1960s with a 30-inch and a 36-inch natural gas line. It is being redistributed here for storage in Pennsylvania and final usage in the New York metropolitan area. (Photograph courtesy of the Williams Corp.)

T.M. Long Co., Inc., located on Pleasant Run Road in Neshanic Station, was started in 1967. This firm supplies proprietary laboratory research instruments to firms around the world. About 50 percent of the products goes to U.S. corporations such as DuPont, Eastman, Exxon, Shell, etc. Thirty percent goes to Japan, and the remainder goes to Europe. (Photograph by G.W. Amerman.)

Foothill Acres Nursing Home, on Amwell Road in Neshanic, was started in 1954 by Dr. Samuel H. Husted. This aerial view shows the facility in the early 1960s, before the third building and main office were built. (Photograph courtesy of Foothill Acres Nursing Home.)

The Foothill Acres staff (Elsie Lynch, admissions; Varian Quick, treasurer; Dr. S.H. Husted, president; Mrs. Husted; and nursing supervisors) are shown here in an early advertisement. (Photograph courtesy of Foothill Acres Nursing Home.)

S.H. Husted, M.D., who was the medical director of Foothill Acres, is shown here. He once said, "I do not concur with the idea that life begins at eighty, but I do believe that an interesting and enjoyable life can be maintained after eighty in proper surroundings in spite of physical handicaps, which are sometimes concurrent with age." (Photograph courtesy of Foothill Acres.)

Winfield Case is shown here behind his soda fountain and grill counter located at 409 Olive Street. Mr. Case also operated the general store at 211 Pearl Street prior to it becoming the post office. (Photograph courtesy of Gwen Jamele.)

This is a view of the Neshanic Flea Market from the Elm Street Bridge. Started in 1969, the market celebrates its 30th anniversary in 1999. (Photograph by G.W. Amerman.)

Carmen Panarello, a vendor at Neshanic Flea Market, has attended every week since the market started, traveling from Pennsauken, New Jersey. (Photograph by G.W. Amerman.)

Flea market vendors are shown here with a representative display of memorabilia, always a crowd favorite. (Photograph by G.W. Amerman.)

This is a local barbershop, located at 416 Olive Street. This building, shown on page 94 as a Metz Auto Agency, has been used as a poultry house, a radio and TV repair shop, a bakery, a firehouse for the 1929 Pirsch, a barber shop, and as a dwelling. (Photograph by G.W. Amerman.)

The last active general store, located at 419 Olive Street, was built by George Moser as an addition to his home. It is now owned and operated by Sal and Darlene Della Ventura, who purchased it in 1985. (Photograph by G.W. Amerman.)

Don's Service Center, shown in this photograph, is located at 606 Marshall Street. This business, started in 1963, has been operated as a repair and repainting service by Don Crane Sr. and Don Crane Jr. for the last 36 years. It is shown on page 100 as the A. Schenck Bergen Allis Chalmers Machinery Agency. It was also operated by John Agans as a repair shop, and as N & T Repair by Simon Nevius and Raymond Toles. (Photograph by Don Crane Jr.)

# Eight
# RECREATION, LEISURE, AND COMMUNITY ACTIVITIES

Baseball was always a featured sporting event in the rural towns of America before WW II, and for a few years after, until travel and industry changed the character and lifestyle of these communities. Neshanic was no exception. The earliest team photograph was of the 1920 Local Lodge players. The players are shown here as follows: Russell Edgar, Russell Cray, Wes Horner, Fred Allegar, Doug Hoff, George Amerman, Lester Gulick, Maurice Griscom, and David Amerman. (Photograph courtesy of Neshanic Station Historical Society.)

Anne Hausch Thompson and Mary Hausch Sixt are seen here working the ice cream stand at the Neshanic Baseball Field in October 1931. (Photograph courtesy of Mary Hausch Sixt.)

In the days of the dairy farm and the dirt road, horseback riding was another pleasure. Shown here in 1959 are Heidi Schlatter and Stacy Smith mounted on Sham and Pan at the River Edge Stock Farm on River Road. (Photograph courtesy of Heidi Schlatter Saunders.)

The Farmers' Baseball Neshanic Team is seen here seated on the rear steps of the Fairview School (by Marshall Street) in 1934. The players are, from left to right, as follows: (bottom row) Bill Kip, Pete Hausch, George Howiler, Hal McBride, and Herb Thompson; (middle row) Harold Neubeck, PeeWee Austin, Stan Hall, Doug Hoff, Earl Vlerebone, and Junior Hall; (top row) Bob May, George Amerman, Mike Hausch (manager), Harold Docherty, and Vin Savage (umpire). (Photograph courtesy of Mary Hausch Sixt.)

Farmers' Baseball Neshanic Team is shown here in 1935, in new uniforms on the front steps of the Fairview School. The players are, from left to right, as follows: (front row) Harold O'Brien, Harold Docherty, Earl Vlerebone, and Walt Kulaski; (middle row) George Howiler, Bill Kip, Mike Hausch (manager), Stan Hall, and Harold Nedbeck; (back row) Pete Hausch, John Wirzman, and Hal McBride. (Photograph courtesy of Mary Hausch Sixt.)

The Neshanic Social Club Team of 1938 is shown here in front of the grandstand, behind the Fairview School. The players are, from left to right, as follows: (front row) Jack Kalpin, Frank Czech, Adam Kalpin, Ernest Snyder, Alan Cray, Art Beers, William Connett, and Frank Kinney; (back row) Donald Hoff, Cliff Hall, Harold Docherty, Duncan O'Brien, Gus Kowalski, Varian Quick, Harold O'Brien, Fred Peabody, Clarence Runyon, and Art Saunders (manager). (Photograph courtesy of Arthur Saunders.)

Neshanic Little Bigger League Team are shown here playing at Saunders Field, on Woodfern Road, in 1956. The players are, from left to right, as follows: (front row) Don Quick, Tom Tharp, Brud Emery (catcher), Taylor Quick (pitcher), Dennis Peterson, and Jim Covert (batboy); (back row) Bucky Covert, Ken Koteles, Mik Peterson, Jim Bowman, Ted Saunders, Fritz Maier, and Varian Quick (manager). (Players not shown are Reid Saunders, Kevin Morton, Bill Tepper, and Chuck Conover.) (Photograph courtesy of the Quick family.)

This view shows a few anglers trying their luck near the Neshanic dam in 1955. The first day of trout season is always busy on the south branch of the Raritan River. The Neshanic Fire Company Ladies Auxiliary often ran a food stand in the Firemen's Field for the first few weekends of the season. (Photograph courtesy of Walter Kostro.)

Early carp fishing on the south branch of the Raritan River produced this Sunday catch for Chance Titman and his brother Henry, who operated the Neshanic Hotel on Amwell Road at the turn of the century. (Photograph courtesy of L.B. Lane.)

Swimming by the Neshanic dam has long been a pastime for area residents. Prior to the demolition of the dam, the favorite swimming hole was above the dam where leaping off rocks into a 12-foot pool provided endless entertainment on sultry summer days. Those less daring were happily cooled in the more shallow waters below the dam, as seen in this 1948 picture of Daniel Schlatter and a friend. (Photograph courtesy of Heidi Schlatter Saunders.)

Even pets were not beyond taking the plunge! (Photograph courtesy of Heidi Schlatter Saunders.)

Ice-skating was another popular river sport. Shown here in 1965, William Toman shows Carol Amerman the basics. Notice the moms, busy talking their way downstream. (Photograph courtesy of G.W. Amerman.)

Perhaps the most universally popular exercises are walking and, more recently, jogging. Despite ever-multiplying subdivisions, the rural environment of Neshanic remains a haven for morning or afternoon strolls. Shown here, strolling past the original Neshanic Depot, is Heidi Saunders. (Photograph courtesy of Ted Saunders.)

Neshanic firemen have long enjoyed saltwater fishing on the Jersey shore. John O'Brien, Captain Percy Giddes of Waretown, and Larry Lane show off a portion of the day's catch of striped bass. Captain Giddes sailed his wood garvey from 1947 until 1994, and Neshanic men fished with him most of those years. (Photograph courtesy of G.W. Amerman.)

Boy Scout Troop 1776, sponsored by the Neshanic Reformed Church, is seen here marching in colonial attire in the 1979 Memorial Day Parade. (Photograph courtesy of G.W. Amerman.)

Shown here are announcements for dances in the early 1900s. Holcombe's Pavilion is now Murphy's Crocodile Inn (formerly the Neshanic Inn). (Courtesy of Dan Bassuk.)

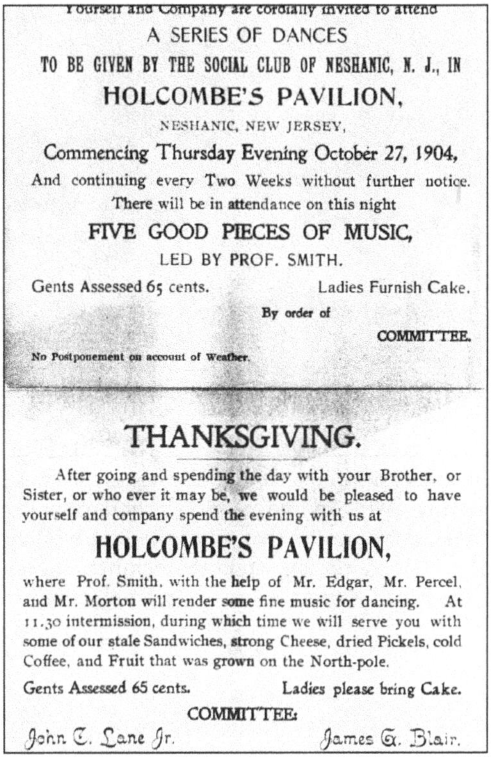

Yourself and Company are cordially invited to attend
A SERIES OF DANCES
TO BE GIVEN BY THE SOCIAL CLUB OF NESHANIC, N. J., IN
**HOLCOMBE'S PAVILION,**
NESHANIC, NEW JERSEY,
Commencing Thursday Evening October 27, 1904,
And continuing every Two Weeks without further notice.
There will be in attendance on this night
**FIVE GOOD PIECES OF MUSIC,**
LED BY PROF. SMITH.

Gents Assessed 65 cents.     Ladies Furnish Cake.

By order of
COMMITTEE.

No Postponement on account of Weather.

---

**THANKSGIVING.**

After going and spending the day with your Brother, or Sister, or who ever it may be, we would be pleased to have yourself and company spend the evening with us at

**HOLCOMBE'S PAVILION,**

where Prof. Smith, with the help of Mr. Edgar, Mr. Percel, and Mr. Morton will render some fine music for dancing. At 11.30 intermission, during which time we will serve you with some of our stale Sandwiches, strong Cheese, dried Pickels, cold Coffee, and Fruit that was grown on the North-pole.

Gents Assessed 65 cents.     Ladies please bring Cake.

COMMITTEE:

John C. Lane Jr.          James G. Blair.

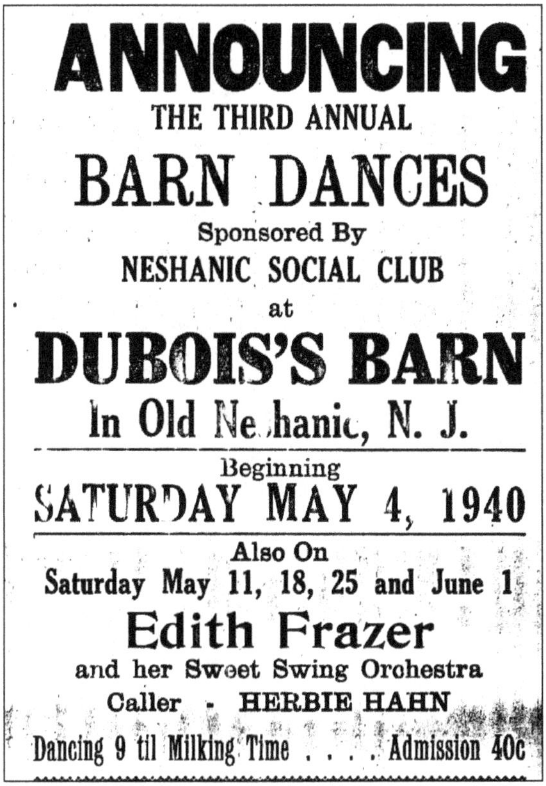

---

**ANNOUNCING**
THE THIRD ANNUAL
**BARN DANCES**
Sponsored By
NESHANIC SOCIAL CLUB
at
**DUBOIS'S BARN**
In Old Neshanic, N. J.

Beginning
SATURDAY MAY 4, 1940
Also On
Saturday May 11, 18, 25 and June 1
**Edith Frazer**
and her Sweet Swing Orchestra
Caller - HERBIE HAHN

Dancing 9 til Milking Time . . . . Admission 40¢

Neshanic Social Club dances were an annual event at the DuBois barn. (Courtesy of Dan Bassuk.)

Members of the Neshanic Garden Club are seen here celebrating the club's 20th anniversary in July 1948. In the caption that appeared with this photograph in the *Plainfield Courier News*, it was noted that 48 of the club's 57 members attended this luncheon at the firehouse. Mrs. Anne Griscom, a charter member, was among those in attendance. The Neshanic Garden Club is still active today. (Photograph courtesy of E. Saums.)

Neshanic Garden Club members are seen here completing work at the sensory garden, which they built in Hillsborough at the Anne Van Middlesworth Park. (Photograph courtesy of Joan Raymond.)

This photograph illustrates the Neshanic Garden Club "Parade of Brides." Many local groups, as well as commercial firms, used the Neshanic Firemen's Hall for a variety of affairs. Before the days of television, the local halls were filled with social activities, including dances, card parties, plays, minstrel shows, and fashion shows. (Photograph courtesy of Phyllis Amerman Polenz.)

Members of the Neshanic J'Avance Club are pictured here in 1949. Organized in 1940, the club was limited to 20 members and met in the members' homes. One program meeting and one recreational evening were held each month. The members also participated in community service and fund-raising activities to benefit local organizations. Members pictured here, from left to right, are as follows: (front row) Miss Myrtle Connet, Mrs. William Campbell, Mrs. Harold Amerman, Miss Virginia Hoff, Mrs. Charles A. Zulauf, Mrs. John Schenck, and Mrs. John Merrill; (back row) Mrs. William Kip, Miss Alice Hoagland, Mrs. Michael Kowalski, Miss Elsie Campbell, Mrs. Gilberta Napolitan, Mrs. Edward Stryker, Miss Mary Hastings, Mrs. Gerald Doran, Mrs. Alice McCaleb, Mrs. William Sheppard, Mrs. Richard Tippett, and Mrs. Herman Thompson. (Photograph courtesy of E. Saums.)

### YOU'LL FIND PLENTY OF BARGAINS AND FUN AT THE ANNUAL

# NESHANIC LIONS CLUB BENEFIT AUCTION

### SAT., SEPT. 21, 1968 STARTING AT 10:30 A.M.
### AT
### McNULTA'S BARN ON AMWELL ROAD, NESHANIC, N.J.

(Directions: Drive South on Route 206 to Hillsborough School, turn right on Amwell Road to Corner Store, turn left and continue for about 4 miles to barn.)

## HOUSEHOLD ARTICLES OF ALL KINDS WILL BE OFFERED

### LUNCH BAR, JEWELRY, & BOOK TABLE (RAIN or SHINE)
### AUCTIONEER: Elwood Heller

Shown here is an announcement for a September 1968 Neshanic Lions Club Benefit Auction at McNulta's Barn, 789 Amwell Road. (Photograph courtesy of Neshanic Lions Club.)

The actual Neshanic Lions Club Benefit Auction is represented in this photograph. (Photograph courtesy of the Neshanic Lions Club.)

This photograph illustrates a c. 1955 Greased Pig and Guinea Chase. From the mid-1930s to the mid-1950s, the Greased Pig and Guinea Chase provided an opportunity for local farmers to make donations for the support of the fire company, as well as providing fun for local residents. Farmers donated guinea hens, pigs, and turkeys while participants paid to run in a race for a chance to catch the prize. (Photograph courtesy of the Toles family.)

The Peanut Butter Playhouse, described as "a theater by children for people of all ages," opened in the old firehouse, on Olive Street, in 1978. The float pictured here appeared at the Memorial Day parade of that year. The playhouse was started by four local couples and produced musicals between 1978 and 1982. Auditions attracted hundreds of young performers aged eight to 18 years from across the state, and performances were usually sold out. (Photograph courtesy of Robert Guterl.)

### Program and Cast
## Stumpville Sewin' Circle,
Neshanic Station M. E. Church,

Friday Evening, November 19, 1909.

---

# H. D. AGANS & CO.,
### NESHANIC STATION, N. J.
### A Clean Store with a Clean Stock.

Your money's worth or your money back without question.

### Highest cash price paid for Fresh Eggs.

Orders taken and delivered free of charge.

Agents for the
## Celebrated Bridgeport Standard Paint
### GIVE US A TRIAL.

This is the cover of the program for *Stumpville Sewin' Circle*. (Courtesy of Harold Van Fleet.)

---

# AUNT JULIA'S PEARLS
## A Hope Moulton Comedy
#### Presented by
#### NESHANIC EPWORTH LEAGUERS

### (CHARACTERS)

Mr. Richard Hunter, *a successful business man*............Schenck Bergen
Mrs. Margaret Hunter, *his wife who has lost all interest in her appearance*............Marie Runke
Betty, *Their daughter who isn't backward about speaking her mind*............Ada Smith
Jim, *Their son, who wastes a lot of time tinkering with the family flivver*............Donald Hoff
Claire Nelson, *Jim's fiancee, who has clever ideas*............Grace Doyle
Marmaduke Waldron, *a foppish young man, who appears harmless but isn't*,............Verian Quick
Aunt Julia, *an elderly relative just arrived from India, who isn't all she seems to be*,............William Kip
Mr. William Somers, *Her New York lawyer, who has an observing eye*............Robert May

Time — *The Present*
Place — *Any small suburb.*

### Synopsis

Act I—*Hunters living room, morning*
Act II—*Same, a week later.*
Act III—*Same, early evening two days later.*

This is the cover of the program for *Aunt Julia's Pearls*. (Courtesy of Harold Van Fleet.)

Shown here is the flyer for *St. Patrick's Dance*. (Courtesy of Harold Van Fleet.)

## St. Patrick's Dance

at the
Neshanic Firemen's Hall
Neshanic Station, New Jersey

### FRIDAY EVENING MARCH 25, 1938

Music by
Hi - De - Ho Boy's of Elizabeth

Sponsored By
NESHANIC SOCIAL CLUB

**YOU'RE A SWEETHEART**
Chorus

You're a sweetheart if there ever was one,
If there ever was one it's you.
Life without you was an incomplete dream,
You are ev'ry sweet dream come true;
My search was such a blind one and I was all at sea,
I never thought I'd find one quite so perfect for me.
You're a sweetheart if there ever was one.
If there ever was one it's you.

**I SEE YOUR FACE BEFORE ME**

I see your face before me
Crowding my ev'ry dream
This is your face before me
You are my only Theme
It doesn't matter where you are
I can see how fair you are
I close my eyes and there you are always
If you could share the magic
If you could see me too
There would be nothing tragic
In all my dreams of you
Would that my love could haunt you so
Knowing I want you so
I can't erase your beautiful
Face before me.

Door Prizes :-: Refreshments
DANCING 9 to 1 - ADMISSION 40c

---

## "CIVIL SERVICE"
### or
### "OLD R. F. D."

**An American Drama in Three Acts.**

PRESENTED BY THE
NESHANIC REFORMED CHURCH PLAYERS

CAST OF CHARACTERS:-
(In the order of their appearance)

| | |
|---|---|
| The Mailing Clerk, Simpson Peavy | William Ackerman |
| The Post Master's Daughter, Octavia Reynolds | Mrs. Geo. B. Scholten |
| The Young Money-Order Clerk, Steve Audaine | John Bittle |
| The Post Master, J. L. Reynolds | George Quick |
| Old R. F. D., A Mystery | Herbert Bingham |
| The Country Boy, Goldie Wex | Tom Bray |
| A Collector, Miss Goldstein | Mrs. George Quick |
| A Lady of Importance, Mrs. T. R. Jeffs | Mrs. Herbert Bingham |
| The Plucky Little Stamp-Clerk, Kate Kenyon | Dorothy Van Liew |
| A Hired Girl, Birdie Bivins | Elizabeth Rue |
| The Inspector, B. J. Cochran | John C. Lane |

Time --- The Present.
Place --- A Small City in the Middle West.

Act I– The Work-Room of a Postoffice. The Saturday after Christmas
The Thief.
Act II-- Same as Act I. A Week Later. ........... The Trial.
Act III– Same as Acts I and II The Next Morning. ------The New Life

Shown here is the program for *Civil Service*. (Courtesy of Harold Van Fleet.)

An auxiliary oiler named for the Neshanic River, the USS *Neshanic* was launched at Sparrows Point, Maryland, by Bethlehem Steel. Following shakedown, she sailed from Hampton Roads. (During WW II, auxiliary ships were named for rivers.) In convoy in April 1943, she steamed with a full cargo of petroleum for the Pacific islands. She served in the Solomons, Tarawa, Hawaii, and the Aleutian Islands. Off Saipan, she was hit on deck with a bomb, which injured 33 of her damage control party. Later, she served in Tokyo Bay. On her return to Norfolk, Virginia, she was decommissioned on December 19, 1945, having been awarded nine battle stars during WW II. She was sold to Gulf Oil Corp., and after serving in the Great Lakes, she was eventually scrapped. (Photograph and records from the Office of Chief of Naval Operations, Volume V, 1970. Courtesy of Thomas E. Tisza, who served in the Pacific as chief executive officer aboard Landing Ships.)

www.ingramcontent.com/pod-product-compliance
Lightning Source LLC
Chambersburg PA
CBHW080903100426
42812CB00007B/2142

IMAGES
of America

# NEW MILFORD

# Images of America
# New Milford

Frances L. Smith

Copyright © 2000 by Frances L. Smith
ISBN 978-1-5316-0276-5

Published by Arcadia Publishing
Charleston, South Carolina

Library of Congress Catalog Card Number: 00106461

For all general information contact Arcadia Publishing at:
Telephone 843-853-2070
Fax 843-853-0044
E-mail sales@arcadiapublishing.com
For customer service and orders:
Toll-Free 1-888-313-2665

Visit us on the Internet at www.arcadiapublishing.com

*To my sons, Joseph Martin and Raymond Dunbar,
and my granddaughter, Stephanie.*

On the cover: Pictured at 39 Old Park Lane are members of the Bostwick family, from left to right, S. Edgar Bostwick, Carrie Bostwick Wallace, Mary Bostwick Berry, Mary Doty Bostwick, and Fred Berry. The family is one of the oldest in town; John Bostwick settled in New Milford in 1707.

# Contents

| | | |
|---|---|---|
| Acknowledgments | | 6 |
| Introduction | | 7 |
| 1. | Chief Waraumaug and the First Settlers | 9 |
| 2. | The Schools | 25 |
| 3. | The Heacocks | 45 |
| 4. | Homes, Churches, and Hospitals | 61 |
| 5. | The King Family | 85 |
| 6. | Farming | 91 |
| 7. | A Look Around | 101 |

# Acknowledgments

It is said, "Men as a whole judge more with their eyes than with their hands." I have gained an even greater appreciation for that proverb during the research and writing of this book. I wish to acknowledge my sincere thanks to each and every one who shared family records, photographs, and innumerable private resources. It has been my endeavor to trace family histories in New Milford and to pass them on to our present and future generations.

I would like to give thanks to the following: the Heacock family; Bette-Lou Emmons, who shared so many photographs of New Milford's first settlers; the Bostwicks; Truman Richmond; Merrill Golden; the New Milford Historical Society; Marilyn Whittlesey, historian, whose time and effort will always be remembered; Roderick Clark, Canterbury School's former headmaster; James Hipp; Maryann Cameron; the Reimeridge family; the Kimberly family; Viola Jones; Robert Stack; Raymond Smith; Stuart Halpin; Rolf Hammer; Sue Noble Kustosz, Classic Photography; Ronald Smith; Patrick Maguire, administrative aide to the mayor; Anna Chapin; Iris Randall; Virginia Decker; Claudia DeLeon; the First Congregational Church; Thomasina Carr; Amy Holding, owner of Office Wizards; and my family, who were a continual source of encouragement in the completion of this work.

—F.L.S.

# INTRODUCTION

The Weautenock tribe occupied the land opposite the village of New Milford prior to 1670, when the people of Fairfield and Stratford turned their attention to *Weautenaug*, the Indian name for New Milford, looking for new land for a plantation. The Weautenocks gave the colonists a deed of sale, dated February 8, 1702 or 1703. The first white settler who made New Milford his permanent residence was John Noble Sr. of Westfield, Massachusetts, in 1707. Noble became the first town clerk and surveyor of lands. He died on August 17, 1714. The Noble family were merchants. The second family to settle in New Milford was that of John Bostwick, whose deed was dated December 2, 1707. Bostwick moved to New Milford primarily to go into the tobacco business. He shared in the official work of the plantation and the town. New Milford was incorporated into a colony in 1712.

The Heacock family were descendants of the Pequot and Narragansett tribes. The first black minister of New Milford was Rev. Stephen Heacock. He was involved in the development of New Milford and served on may town committees. The religious leader Rev. Daniel Boardman settled in New Milford in 1715 and established the Congregational church in 1716. The Episcopal church followed. In 1729, civic and educational sites were established at the north end of the town green.

New Milford became a very prosperous business center. It had gristmills, hat and button factories, pottery makers, blacksmiths, and farms, whose main crops were tobacco and wheat. James Hine was the first blacksmith. New Milford Pottery was organized in June 1887, with some 30 residents subscribing to the capital stock. By August 1887, the company had purchased 3 acres of land known as Giddings Mill, where the Robertson Bleachery stands today.

Other places of business included Frederick Boardman's drugstore on the west side of Railroad Street, near the depot; it was stocked with patent medicines of the time. On the south corner of Wall and Railroad Streets was F.G. Bennett and Son furniture store and undertaking business. Daniel Marsh and his son T.T. Marsh ran a coal yard near the depot. Harvey Jennings opened a grocery and confectionery in 1847. Mrs. Stephen Wells was a milliner.

In 1852, Albert S. Hill and Edward Barton built a paper mill on the East Aspetuck River, a mile above Northville; the mill converted straw and rags into straw-board paper that was used for hatboxes and dry goods boxes. Sylvanus Merwin operated a hotel at Gaylord's Ville; at that time, the stop on the railroad was called Merwinsville. Merwin held a contract that required every train to stop at Merwinsville so that passengers might eat or spend the night at his hotel.

Brothers William W. and Edwin S. Wells ran a gristmill on the river. Charles G. Peck was a harness maker. William B. Wright sold stoves, plumbing, and tinware. In the Maryland district, Roswell, Sheldon, and David Northrup operated a foundry and machine shop, making castings to order, iron fences, and machinery.

Bridgewater was a part of New Milford until 1856. Smith and Erwin opened a hat factory in Bridgewater in 1834; they moved their factory to New Milford in 1855. In the the 1880s, the Conetia Wheel Club became popular; residents used bicycles to visit a neighbor or go to the store, but the real fun was in getting a crowd together and going for a spin.

The Fugitive Slave Act of 1850 brought the question of slavery to every mind and resulted in the Underground Railroad, which allowed at least 20,000 Negroes to escape. In New Milford and in nearby Washington, there were active sympathizers for this cause.

The first meeting of the Housatonic Agricultural Society was held in Wright's Hall in 1858. The first fairs in New Milford were held on a lot behind the residence of Dr. James Hine. Later, the Fair Committee rented the grounds of F.S. Richmond, a few miles south of the village, on the west side of the Housatonic River, northwest of the Indian Burying Grounds.

Levi S. Knapp's barbershop on Bank Street was named Topeka Hall for the Kansas-Nebraska troubles of the 1850s. For more than 50 years, the hall was an almost nightly gathering place for the men of the town to play heated games of checkers, interspersed with good talk.

Brothers-in-law Merritt Beach and Alanson Canfield opened the town's first lumberyard; it was located on Elm Street at the former site of St. Francis Xavier Church. One of the few industries in the area at the end of the nineteenth century was the Bridgeport Wood Finishing Company, which was located on the Still River in the Lanesville section of New Milford.

For the past 40 years, the Kimberly-Clark Corporation has been New Milford's largest employer and taxpayer. Selectman E. Paul Martin played a major role in bringing Kimberly-Clark to town. To convince the corporation that New Milford was the place to build a new plant, Martin traveled to company headquarters in Wisconsin with with Gov. Abraham Ribicoff and George DeVoe, president of the New Milford Chamber of Commerce.

As time has gone by, New Milford has developed in new and different ways. However, as you walk or drive by the historic areas and along the country roads, keep in mind the photographs in this book and search for a glimpse of the past from which we came.

—Fran Smith

# One

# CHIEF WARAUMAUG AND THE FIRST SETTLERS

Waraumaug, the last chief of the Weautenock tribe, died c. 1735. He was buried on the mountain near the place where he had resided for so long. A pile of stones on an open plot of ground marks the place where his remains repose. The original pile was formed as each of the warriors who belonged to the tribe deposited a stone upon the grave. In the years that followed, members of the tribe continued this custom, placing another stone on the grave each time they visited it. In the 1880s, a family from Bridgeport bought the land and utilized the stones from the monument for the foundation and chimney of a pseudo-castle that was built for them.

George Henry Noble, son of Ezra Noble, was born in New Milford on March 12, 1814. He was a descendant of New Milford's first settler, John Noble Sr. George Noble served as postmaster from 1853 to 1856 and was a delegate to the national convention that nominated Abraham Lincoln for president in 1860. An influential member of the Congregational church, Noble died on December 10, 1872, at age 58.

Pictured at 39 Old Park Lane are members of the Bostwick family, from left to right, S. Edgar Bostwick, Carrie Bostwick Wallace, Mary Bostwick Berry, Mary Doty Bostwick, and Fred Berry. The family is one of the oldest in town; John Bostwick settled in New Milford in 1707.

The Benjamin Bostwick farm was located at Squire Hill and Cherniske Road in Merryall.

Mary Doty Bostwick leans on her elbow and looks up from the pages in front of her for a moment. She wears a long-sleeved, high-collared dress and an ornament in her hair. A housewife, she was born in 1846 and died in 1919.

Lile Bostwick was the daughter of Addie Strong. In 1924, she donated her home on Elm Street to the New Milford Hospital. The house had room for 24 patients.

Wearing hats that offer some shade, Mary Bostwick Berry and her mother, Mary Doty Bostwick, share a restful moment at Lake Waraumaug in New Preston. Mary Bostwick Berry was born on August 1, 1873. She married Fred Berry on October 12, 1897. She died on March 25, 1955, at the age of 81.

Enjoying the air on the porch c. the 1890s are, from left to right, Martha Stone, three Simpson children, Winnie Simpson, Mary Doty Bostwick holding her dog, and another Simpson boy.

13

William Bostwick, pictured in uniform at age 18, was born on September 5, 1865, the eldest son of Mary Doty Bostwick. He built the "Bit of Country" house. On October 18, 1893, he married Lottie Root of Bridgeport, and the couple had three children: Lottie May, Raymond William, and Nathan Bostwick. He died on November 14, 1957, at the age of 92.

This photograph shows eldest son William Bostwick in his forties. He is still wearing a mustache.

Edward C. Howland (standing) built the house on Old Park Lane where Bette-Lou Emmons now resides. Born in 1877, Howland married Anne Bostwick on September 26, 1900. The couple had two children: Harriet May in 1903 and Jessie L. Howland (Emmons) in 1911. The two seated gentlemen in this late-nineteenth-century photograph could not be identified.

Cyrus Bostwick was another member of the New Milford Bostwick family. Born on May 31, 1836, he left Connecticut to go to Oregon. There, he became involved in the fishing industry and grew very prosperous. He married Sarah Riblet on June 15, 1864. Members of their family still live in Oregon.

In this mid-1890s view, the husband sits and the wife stands at his side. The couple are William Bostwick and Lottie Root Bostwick. They were married on October 18, 1893.

This happy looking two-year-old is Nathan Bostwick, son of William and Lottie Bostwick. He lived in the Bostwick house called "Bit of Country." The photograph dates from c. 1905.

Anne Bostwick Howland, at age 20, sits on a stone wall across from the Emmons (Howland) House on Park Lane. The photograph was taken in 1896. Today, the field remains the same.

Ready for a carriage ride in 1890 are, from left to right, Mary Jane Angus, Mary Bostwick, Anne Bostwick, Lyla Bostwick, and Em Bostwick.

Sarah "Sate" Bostwick married Dr. Frederick King in 1899. The couple lived on Bridge Street in a house that is now the Mini Mart Store.

The Bostwick sisters pose for a picture in 1876. On the left at age ten is Sara "Sate" Bostwick. On the right at age seven is Emily Bostwick. Born in July 1869, Emily Bostwick became a Christian Science practitioner in New Milford. She died in 1956.

Among the family members pictured outside in the sun at the Bostwick Homestead c. 1900 are the following: (front row) Emily Bostwick, Amy Bostwick, and grandmother Mary Doty Bostwick, holding her dog; (back row) Fred Berry, husband of Mary Bostwick, wearing a bonnet; William Bostwick, standing the doorway; and Anne Bostwick. The children are Arthur Bostwick's.

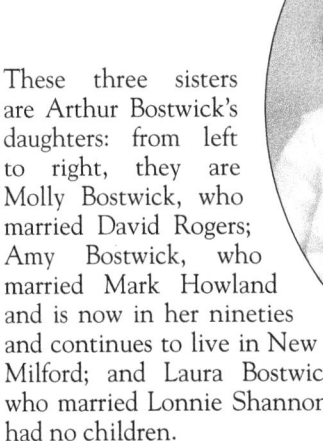

These three sisters are Arthur Bostwick's daughters: from left to right, they are Molly Bostwick, who married David Rogers; Amy Bostwick, who married Mark Howland and is now in her nineties and continues to live in New Milford; and Laura Bostwick, who married Lonnie Shannon and had no children.

A very attentive fox studies Lillian Turrell, who has the animal on a leash. The fox was caught inside the Turrell home on Old Park Lane c. the early 1900s.

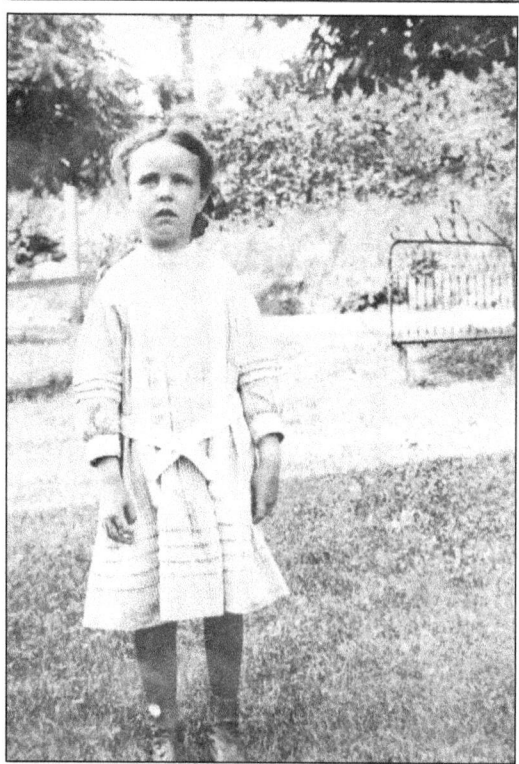

Harriet May Howland is pictured at age five in the yard of her family's home on Wellsville Avenue in 1908. She never married.

These three sisters are the children of Mary Bostwick Berry and Fred Berry, and the granddaughters of Mary Doty Bostwick. Pictured in 1909, from left to right, they are Dorothy, Mary, and Flora Berry.

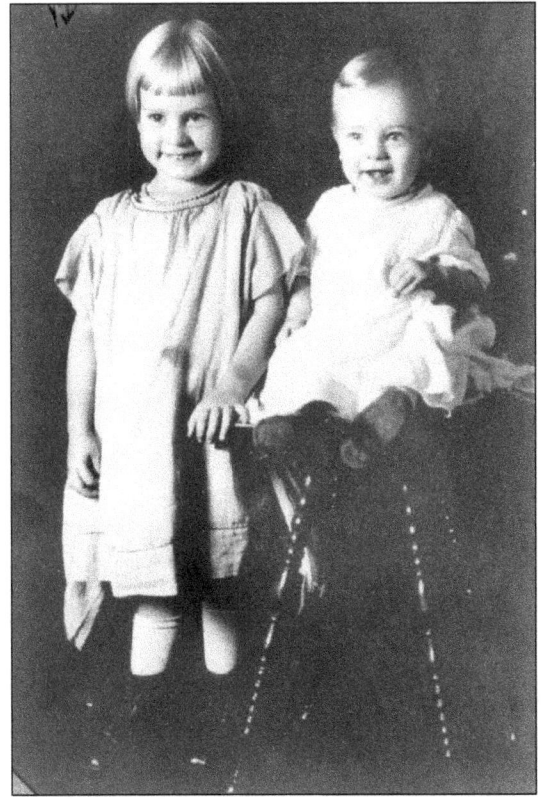

Jean and Raymond "Bud" Bostwick, grandchildren of William Bostwick, smile brightly as their picture is taken. Bud Bostwick, who lived on Crossman Road, died early in the summer of 2000.

This 1897 photograph shows Arthur Bostwick at age 21. Notice his fancy shirt and tie.

At age 15, Edgar Bostwick sits atop a stone wall c. 1898, dressed in his best suit and cap.

Focusing their attention on two different things, the little dog and the little girl remain in place long enough for this photograph to be taken in 1906. The girl is Harriet May Howland, age 3, eldest daughter of Anne Bostwick Howland.

Fancy hats were in vogue for the New Milford Bicentennial Celebration in 1907. Posing on the occasion of the town's 200th anniversary are the following, from left to right: (front row) Minnie Sullivan, Dorothy Berry, Georgia Johnson, Vera Leavenworth, Ruth Sullivan, Lottie May Bostwick, Genevieve Crane, May Bostwick, Esther Carlson, three unidentified young women, Elizabeth Sullivan, unidentified, and Morse Leavensworth; (back row) Ray Bostwick, Dolly Stone, Jerry Northrop, unidentified, Mary Leavenworth, six unidentified young people, Elizabeth Graham, ? Edwards, Eula Dunlap, and George Sullivan.

This is Solomon Edgar Bostwick in 1903. He married Marion Wooster, and they had two children, Robert and Betty Bostwick.

Sisters Laura (left) and Amy Bostwick, daughters of Arthur Bostwick, wear similar dresses, wristwatches, and hairdos.

# Two

# THE SCHOOLS

This is the Main House at Canterbury School. Nelson Hume and Henry O. Havemeyer founded the school in 1915. Their vision was an upstart: first, because they wanted a school free of the anti-Catholic prejudice that they had experienced at boarding schools, universities, and other institutions of higher learning; second, because they decided to use laymen as teachers, while keeping the school within the Catholic tradition. Among those who attended Canterbury, with its high standard of learning, are John Carroll, John F. Kennedy, and Mario Cuomo.

## PROGRAMME

The National Anthem

The Headmaster's Address

The Presentation of Diplomas

The Address to the Graduates
By James A. Farrell, Esq.

The Award of Prizes

The Giving of the Blessing
By His Eminence John Cardinal Farley
Archbishop of New York

The Closing Hymn

CLASS OF 1918

CYRIL HUME
GEORGE FROST McLAUGHLIN
SWITHIN JOSEPH NICHOLS
ARTHUR EDWARD O'GORMAN

## CANTERBURY SCHOOL
### Programme of the First Graduation Exercises
NEW MILFORD        JUNE THE EIGHTH 1918

This is the program for the first graduation exercises at Canterbury School, held on June 8, 1918. Listed as members of the graduating class are Cyril Hume, George Frost McLaughlin, Swithin Joseph Nichols, and Arthur Edward O'Gorman. James A. Farrell, Esq., gave the address to the graduates, and his Eminence John Cardinal Farley, archbishop of New York, gave the blessing.

This photograph shows students and faculty members at Canterbury School in 1924, nine years

The Carriage House still stands on the Canterbury School campus, but it is in need of repair.

after the founding of the school in 1915 by Nelson Hume and Henry O. Havemeyer.

This c. 1900s view focuses on the northeast corner of Hickory Hearth at Canterbury School, where two young men are having a conversation.

The Bungalow at Canterbury School was used for students and guests. It was destroyed by fire in December 1925.

This is an interior view of the Main House at Canterbury School. The house was built in 1915 and was decorated with period pieces. The upstairs floor contained rooms for students and an apartment for guests.

Founded by Sarah Black in 1899, the Ingleside School was a boarding school for young ladies. This view shows the Old Middle House, which was destroyed by fire, rebuilt, and reopened in 1938. Today, the Old Middle House is part of Canterbury School.

In 1847, Ambrose S. Rogers opened the Adelphic Institute in North Cornwall as an English and classical school for boys. In 1860, he moved the school to New Milford. He built a large house and school building on 20 acres of land southeast of the village. Students came from all sections of the United States, from the West Indies, and from South America. During the Civil War, Adelphic became a military school and several of its students became officers in the U.S. Army. In all, 500 students attended the institute before it closed in 1876. Rogers died in 1882.

These are the students at St. Francis School in 1938. The students are pictured on the lawn in front of the school.

Pictured outside the Main Street School in 1941 is the second-grade class. The boy second from the left in the middle row is Larry Emmons.

The public schoolhouse was completed in 1876 on East Street. It was organized as a grade school, with four teachers. It had all the modern conveniences, including a library with 600 volumes.

This was a New Milford High School basketball team. The last names of these players are as follows, from left to right: (front row) Straub, Kohne, Leahey, Dorwin, Roscoe, Warner, and Kibbe; (back row) Peagler, Kwasniewski, Tanner, and Lane.

The New Milford High School Class of 1929 started with 83 members. Larry Lillis, shown in the first row on the right, was voted the most popular student.

Posing for this photograph is the New Milford High School Class of 1921. The graduating class stands on the steps of the library.

New Milford Center High School was located on Main Street. The original school was attended by Clement H. Noble, Betty Noble, and John Noble, descendants of New Milford's first settler, John Noble Sr. The school became a grade school, for students in first through eighth grades. It was later torn down to make way for Main Street School, which is next to the Congregational church.

Students and faculty member of New Milford High School gather to have their picture taken outdoors in May 1920. Pictured in the photograph below with his arms folded at the far left is

Joe Lillis. The light-haired man standing in front of the doors is John Pettibone.

Robert Ohmen was unanimously elected president of the New Milford High School Class of 1931. He was considered the best all-around person in the senior class.

Among the class officers at New Milford High School are four serving the Class of 1931: Robert Ohmen, class president, front row, fourth from left;. Stuart Lathrop, vice president; Clifford Kiefer, secretary; and Reginald Taylor, treasurer.

This photograph shows the administration and faculty of New Milford High School in 1931. Pictured, from left to right, are the following, with only last names given: (front row) Wells, Bousquet, Pettibone, Couch, and Knox; (back row) Erwin, Sullivan, Tonkin, Millane, Perry, Campbell, and Lumley.

Pictured in 1934 are the administration and faculty of New Milford High School. The last names of the members shown, from left to right, are as follows: (front row) Haas, Merwin, Couch, Pettibone, Welsh, Campbell, and Myers; (middle row) Lynch, Lillis, Perry, Carney, and Sullivan; (back row) Hunt, Knox, Wells, Neidel, and Lamiey.

Standing in the doorway with two other young ladies is Catherine Lillis, left, who served as vice principal of the John Pettibone School. Note the large amount of snow still on the ground. Today, this building is called the Richmond Center.

Students and faculty of New Milford High School assemble for a photograph in 1926. The young men are shown above and most of the young women are pictured below.

This is the New Milford High School basketball team of 1928–1929. Larry Lillis stands in the back row at the left. The team played hard and won many games. Notice the players' sneakers.

## Three

# THE HEACOCKS

Richard Heacock was born in New Milford in 1818. He served in the 29th Colored Volunteers, and his name appears on the monument on the New Milford Green. His wife, Hannah, also was born in New Milford. Both husband and wife were descendants of the Pequot and Narragansett Indians. He died in 1868 at age 50; she died in 1888.

Rev. Stephen Heacock served as recording secretary of the Colored People's Temperance Union of New Milford. He and his family are pictured in 1912 in front of the homestead on Old State Road. They are, from left to right, the following: (front row) Reverend Heacock, son Stewart Heacock, and wife, Mary Gregory Heacock; (back row) Charles Freeman, Roland Heacock, Martha Benson, Granville Heacock, Steve Heacock, Mabel Heacock, and Sue Freeman.

Stephen Heacock was publicly ordained to the ministry by the speaker and associates of the Ministers' Board of Conference on November 11, 1897, at the New Milford Town Hall. He became pastor of the Advent Christian Church of New Milford, organized on February 20, 1900, with 22 members. The church building pictured was erected on Brookside Avenue in 1901. Its bell was a gift from a Mr. Shonio, who presented it in memory of the tragic incidents of the Old French and Indian War. The bell was christened "Sansaman" in honor of the first Christian missionary of New England killed by King Philip of the Wampanoags in 1675. The bell was donated to the New Milford Historical Society by the Heacock family as part of the history of New Milford.

The Rev. Dr. Roland T. Heacock was the son of Rev. Stephen Heacock and Mary Gregory Heacock. Born in New Milford on December 30, 1893, he graduated from Howard University in 1921 and from Yale Divinity School in 1924. He received his master's degree in sacred theology in 1926 and a doctor of divinity degree from American International College. He married Lucille LaCour and had three children: Donald, Lucille, and Joan. In 1959, Heacock became one of the first black ministers to serve an all-white congregation when he assumed the pastorate of Staffordville Congregational Church in Stafford Springs. His children grew up to become Dr. Donald Heacock, Lucille Heacock Layton, and Joan Heacock Ghebreeschel. The pastor died in 1972.

Tilman Heacock was born in New Milford. He went into the dry cleaning and the wood business. He also built homes and painted pictures, which were displayed in his home.

Hannah Heacock, wife of Richard Heacock, holds her son Tilman, who is just one year old.

Mary Gregory Heacock, wife of Stephen Heacock, sits with her sons around her. The sons are, from left to right, Roland, Steve, and Granville Heacock. The photograph was taken in the yard of the Heacock Homestead on Old State Road in 1912.

Rev. Stephen Heacock sits with his three daughters in 1912. The daughters are, from left to right, Martha Heacock Benson, Susie Heacock Freeman, and Mabel Galena Heacock.

Three couples stand outside the Granville Heacock home on Elm Street Extension. They are, from left to right, Net and Tilman Heacock, Ett and Granville Heacock, and the Rices from New Britain.

Alvira Heacock Killingsworth was the daughter of Alfred and Elizabeth Benson Heacock. Born in New Milford on March 29, 1894, she was a descendant of the Pequot and the Scaticook Indians and spoke the language of the tribes. She attended New Milford schools.

Mildred Heacock was the daughter of Alfred and Elizabeth Benson Heacock. Born in New Milford, she attended New Milford schools. She was one of the first blacks to graduate from Bellevue Hospital School of Nursing in New York City. Because of her light skin color, she was in the white class.

Alvira Heacock Killingsworth, the daughter of Alfred and Elizabeth Benson Heacock, is pictured here in 1913 at the age of 21 before she left for California. She lived to be 105 years old, dying in 1997.

This photograph of a New Milford class was taken approximately 100 years ago. Alvira Heacock Killingsworth is in the third row, fourth from the left. Others pictured include Julia Cogswell, Otto Curry, and Kathleen Buffett.

These sisters are the children of Alfred and Elizabeth Benson Heacock. Pictured in 1901, they are sitting in a field of wildflowers at the Sherman home of their maternal grandfather, Minot Benson. They are, from left to right, Cora, Alvira, Ethel, and Mildred Heacock.

Outside Granville Heacock's house on Elm Street Extension are seven friends. Among those pictured with Granville and Ett Heacock in the late 1800s are Net and Tilman Heacock and the Rices of New Britain.

This house on Elm Street Extension is the home of William Alfred Heacock Jr.

Sally Benson was the sister of Elizabeth Benson Heacock. This photograph was taken in 1904.

Nellie Brooks was born in New Milford c. the 1890s. She was the second wife of Granville Heacock.

Pictured c. the late 1800s are Elizabeth Heacock Wheeler, left, and Nellie Heacock Bailey. Elizabeth Heacock married Walter Wheeler of New Milford. She had two sons, Walter and Arthur Wheeler. Both sons served in the Spanish-American War. Arthur Wheeler was lost in the war. Walter Wheeler was a Buffalo soldier and served as a special scout with Theodore Roosevelt's Rough Riders. He returned to New Milford and later moved to California. Nellie Heacock was born in New Milford. She married Mr. Bailey, and the couple lived in New Milford.

Minot Benson was the father of Elizabeth Benson Heacock. He was an English settler who moved to Sherman. He married an Indian woman.

Mrs. Minot Benson was the mother of Elizabeth Benson Heacock. She was born in New Milford and was a descendant of the Pequot, Narragansett, and Scaticook tribes.

Star Benson was the brother of Elizabeth Benson Heacock.

Martha Heacock Benson was the eldest daughter of Rev. Stephen Heacock and Mary Heacock. Born c. 1877, she is pictured here in the 1890s. She made a living crocheting tablecloths for people in New Milford. She died in July 1969 at the age of 92.

Ett Heacock was the wife of Granville Heacock. She was very fashionable and wore the latest style clothing. This photograph was taken in the 1890s.

Pictured in the 1890s are Mabel Galena Heacock, left, and her aunt Ett Heacock. Mabel Heacock was the daughter of Rev. Stephen Heacock and Mary Heacock. She was born in New Milford on March 25, 1889. She enjoyed cooking and had a winning personality.

# Four

# HOMES, CHURCHES, AND HOSPITALS

New Milford's bandstand was built in 1896. It was originally placed farther north on the town green. It survived the fire of 1902. The bandstand housed a barbershop until Bank and Railroad Streets could be rebuilt. On November 27, 1852, the Town appointed a committee of five to choose a site for the new town hall. Two proposals were required. C.S. Roberts was chosen as architect and the New Milford Town Hall was built in 1875 at a cost of $26,000 on what was formerly the site of the Roger Sherman Home. From 1837 to 1882, the building that became the Village Hardware Store served as the third home of St. John's Episcopal Church. When the church moved to its present home in 1882, the building was remodeled and the steeple was removed. It became a hard goods store, which also sold wood wagons and farm supplies. The present owners are Tom and Barbara Leahy. The store is in the process of becoming an antique mall.

Levi Sydney Knapp was a shoemaker by trade. This photograph was taken in 1870.

Daniel Burritt built this house c. 1770. In 1838, the house became the home of the Knapp family. The Knapps moved to New Milford from Stratford. Mary Clissold Knapp, the last living member of the family, gave the home to the New Milford Historical Society with the provision that the home be restored.

This photograph of the Park View House on Bridge Street dates from c. 1900. Ithnar and Bessie Canfield built the house in 1823 for their son Royal S. Canfield and his wife. In 1871, Merritt Beach purchased the house and, over the next 40 years, leased it and operated it as a boardinghouse—first as the Wheaton House and then as the Park View House. In 1910, C.M. Beach remodeled the house as a Greek Revival-style residence. The house is now the Lillis Funeral Home.

This photograph shows the Lillis Funeral Home.

This picture of the Wayside Inn was taken in 1905. The inn catered to many travelers who came into the area.

At the time this photograph was taken in 1898, the house shown was 100 years old. It was the home of Tommy Wells. Edwin Bostwick later purchased it. The two women in the carriage are Anne and Mary Doty Bostwick.

In 1788, Nicholas Wanzer deeded land to the Quakers. It is the same land on which the Quaker Meeting House still stands, complete with the adjoining burying grounds. The old Quaker Meeting House was removed to the site from the Pickett district.

Elisha Bostwick built the Bostwick House on Grove Street. He acquired the property upon his return from the Revolutionary War. The house was completed in 1782. Bostwick served as the town clerk for 55 years; he also was a justice of the peace, a land surveyor, and a colonel in the state militia. In the mid-1800s, the Bostwick House was a station on the Underground Railroad.

This photograph of Maplewood on Park Lane was taken in 1905. Maplewood was an inn for travelers. It later became the Bostwick Homestead.

Located on Park Lane, this is currently the home of Bette-Lou Emmons. The barn on the right is the stable for her Lipizzaner stallions. The photograph was taken in 1896.

This bird's-eye view of New Milford was taken looking toward the Kimberly-Clark Corporation, which for the past 40 years has been the town's largest employer and taxpayer.

Originally, this house on Main Street belonged to Solomon Edgar Bostwick. Bostwick built the house c. 1905.

These two photographs are of house that was once owned by Walter Bostwick and later owned by the Nettleton family. The view above shows the front entrance of the house. The side view, below, was taken just before the house was torn down in 1959.

This 1910 picture shows Bank Street, looking west. The Slone Pharmacy is to the right on the corner. Notice the streetlights.

This is the present town library. The first library in New Milford was established in 1796. At that time, the collection of more than 355 volumes was housed in private homes. Later, the New Milford Library Association opened a library in the town hall. Later still, Egbert Marsh donated land and the association built the first public library. The Egbert Marsh Memorial Library, the small building on the left, was used until the library outgrew it. The building then became the home of Col. William J. Starr.

St. John's Episcopal Church was built in 1882. Gothic in style, the church was constructed of native stone and granite. The parish house was completed in 1959.

Charles Starr built this structure on Bridge Street in the 1840s for use as a tobacco warehouse. William and Sherman Green purchased the property in 1908. The Green Warehouse sold house supplies, farming equipment, as well as general lawn and garden needs and coal. The porch of the building was always graced with a white horse—a landmark. At the present time, the building is the Heritage Inn of Litchfield County.

This house in Merryall was the homestead of Epenatus Platt, who is is buried in the upper Merryall Cemetery. The photograph was taken in the late 1800s.

The Berry Homestead was located at 49 Park Lane Road (Route 202), on the corner of Park Lane West. It was sold to Bette-Lou Emmons in 1967 and then to Jack Gulliver in 1971. Later, it was destroyed by fire.

The old Boardman Home on Main Street was given to the New Milford Historical Society. This photograph was taken in 1959. The house was torn down in 1965 to make way for further land development.

This photograph shows the upper east side of the green. The brick building is the first high school in New Milford. The second building is the Hine House, built c. 1843, which is now the private home and offices of attorneys John and Suzanne Powers. The third house belonged to Dr. George Taylor and had an unclear history. It is currently the private law office of Moots, Pellegrini, Spillane, & Mannion.

This is the south view of Solomon Edgar Bostwick's house. The house to the right is the home of Walter Bostwick.

The Bostwick Homestead graces this land. The two women entering the gate are Mary Doty Bostwick and her daughter.

This 1908 photograph shows South Main Street. The Webster Bank currently owns the house on the left. The house on the right was torn down, and the Fleet Bank building now occupies that site.

This photograph of Main Street was taken looking south in 1908. The New Milford Green is still one of the loveliest greens in the country.

Rev. Noah Porter, D.D., L.L.D, served as pastor of the New Milford Congregational Church from 1836 to 1843. In later years, he became the president of Yale College, a position that he held from 1871 to 1886.

The Congregational church was organized on November 21, 1716, with 13 members. The first church was built between 1718 and 1719 and was opened in 1720. Drums called people to worship. A second church was built in 1754. Pictured is the present Federal-style First Congregational Church, which was built in 1833. The steeple of the church contains a 1905 Seth Thomas Clock made in Thomaston. The Jones Bell Company manufactured the steeple bell in 1880.

In the 1960s, the Old Northville Church was moved from its original site next to the post office down the road to a new location. The original building, the center of community life for many years, still stands; however, a new church was built at 9 Little Bear Hill.

The Merryall Chapel, built December 18, 1890, is one of the oldest churches in the area. It still stands on this country road in Merryall.

In the early 1700s, Nicolas Wanzer deeded land to the Quakers. It is the same land on which the old Quaker Meeting House now stands, with the burial grounds adjoining. The old Quaker House was moved here from the Pickett district.

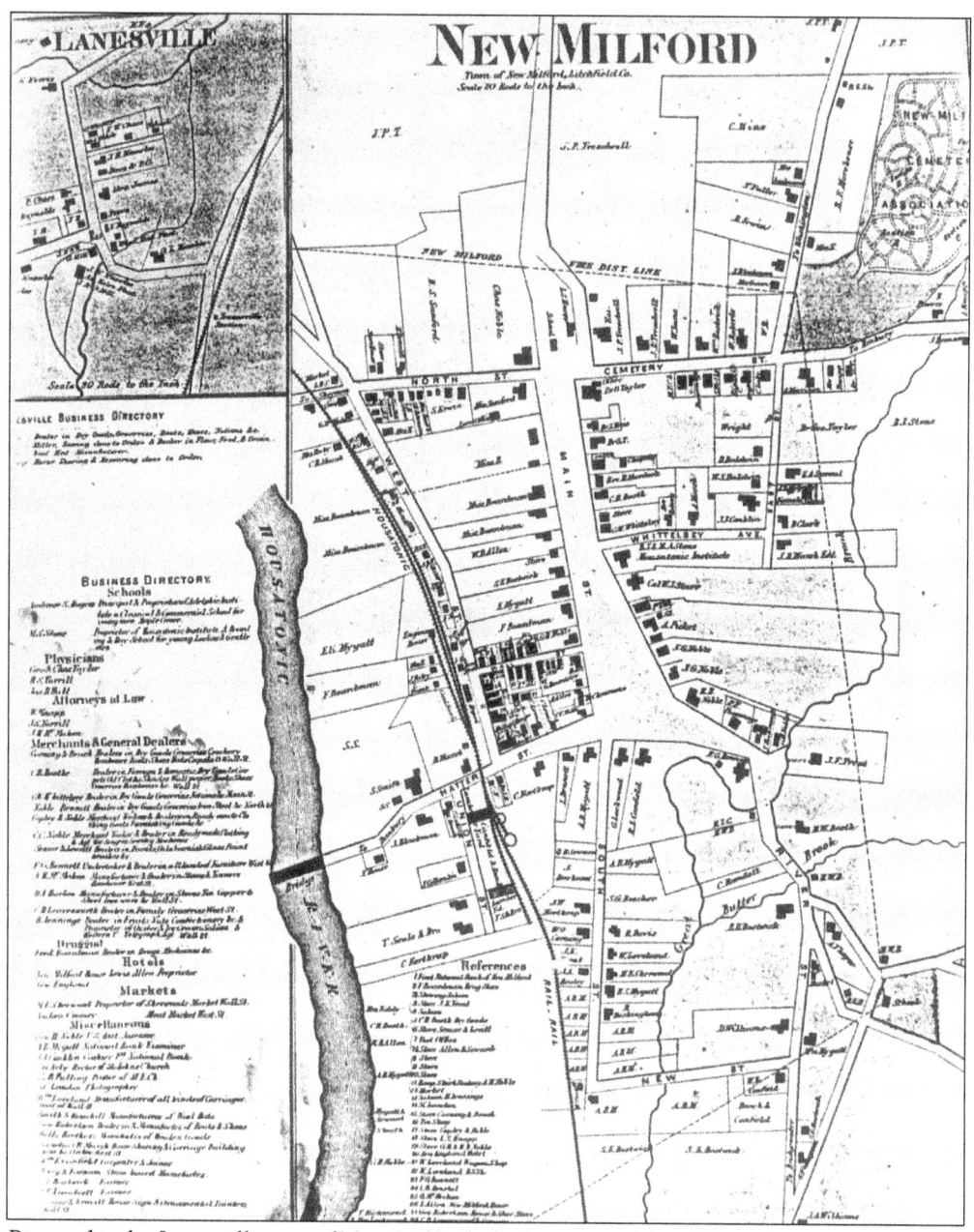

Pictured is the Lanesville area of New Milford, the location of the old Quaker Church.

Ada Ducksworth, who came to the United States from England, married Alfred C. Worley in the late 1800s.

Alfred Worley, husband of Ada Ducksworth Worley, bought the *New Milford Gazette* and changed its name to the *New Milford Times*. The Worleys had four children: George, Harry, Philip, and Ethel. For 50 years, Harry "Sandy" Worley wrote the *Times* column "Sandy Sez."

The first New Milford Hospital was on Whittlesey Avenue. It consisted of a 10-bed institution in a house that was owned by a Mrs. Robert P. Strong. When the hospital moved to larger quarters on Elm Street, Dr. Ruppert Day purchased the property on Whittlesey Avenue for his home and lived there for 46 years.

In 1924, Lile Bostwick donated her home on Elm Street to the New Milford Hospital. The hospital had the capacity to handle 24 patients.

The medical staff of the New Milford Hospital included, from left to right, the following:(front row) Dr. C. George Lataif, Dr. ? Opper, Dr. Howard G. Stevens, Dr. Robert S. Day, Dr. Richard Ireland, and Dr. William Dobbs; (back row) Dr. Warren G. Koehler, Dr. John Simonds, Dr. ? Wolfe, Dr. Howard S. Morrow, and Dr. John Street.

Looking south from the bridge along Route 7, this view shows the 1948 flood of the Housatonic River.

An earlier flood of the Housatonic River occurred in 1936. Don Emmons indicates the high-water mark outside the Socony gas station.

New Milford Hospital cofounder Mrs. Robert P. Strong not only helped establish the town's first hospital but also served as its first treasurer for 46 years. She retired on October 25, 1967.

New Milford Hospital cofounder Robert S. Day, M.D., graduated from New York Medical College in 1906. After graduating he moved to Bridgewater, where he practiced for one year. In 1910, he came to New Milford and became the hospital's first surgeon.

This photograph shows the present new New Milford Hospital, an affiliate of Columbia Presbyterian Medical Center. The hospital is located on 21 Elm Street Extension.

Members of the General Committee for the town's 250th anniversary meet in 1956. They are, from left to right, the following: (front row) Fred Planz, Charles D. Couch, Howard Peck, Adaline Strong, and Merrill S. Golden; (back row) Joseph Smith, E. Paul Martin, Mrs. John Duris, Harold Hunt, Alice Kewnel, Doris Warwick, Henry Smithwick, Lillian Corey, C. Robert Ohmen, and Clifford Kiefer.

# *Five*
# THE KING FAMILY

Taken during graduation exercises of the New Milford High School Class of 1907, this photograph shows Eugenia King, the only child of Dr. Frederick King and his wife, Sarah Bostwick King. Eugenia King is in the back row, third from the left. She was born on January 25, 1890, with a heart condition that resulted in her death at the age of 21 years.

This is a mid-1800s photograph of the father of Dr. Frederick S. King.

Pictured in the mid-1800s is the mother of Dr. Frederick S. King.

This 1895 photograph shows Eugenia King, age 5, with her father and mother, Dr. Frederick King and Sarah Bostwick King.

This picture was taken in Dr. Frederick King's medical office on Bridge Street in 1899. It shows Dr. Frederick King, his wife, Sarah Bostwick King, and their daughter, Eugenia King.

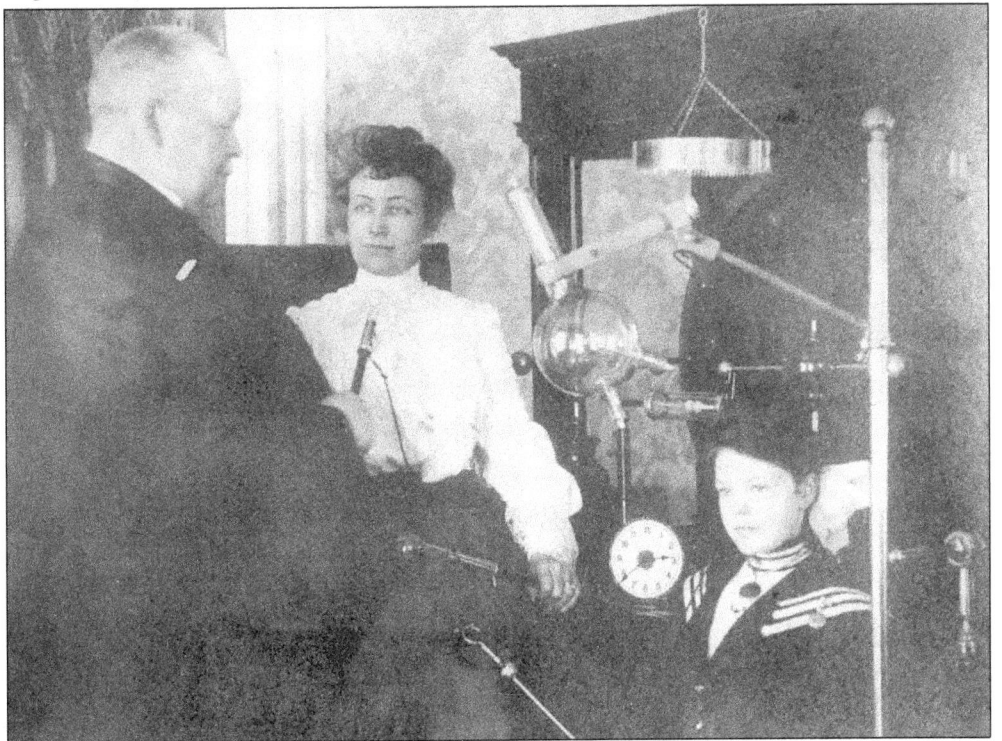

Eugenia King was born on September 17, 1891. She was about ten years of age when this photograph was taken. Notice her stylish dress.

Eugenia King participated in a May Day celebration in New Milford when she was nine years old. The lovely dress, jewelry, and flowers suited her perfectly.

Pictured in 1912 is Eugenia King, the daughter of Dr. Frederick and Sarah King. Eugenia King died later that year, at age 21.

Dr. and Mrs. Frederick King gave the baptismal font at the New Milford Congregational Church in memory of their daughter, Eugenia King, shown at age 21.

Sarah Bostwick King was born in New Milford. She married Dr. Frederick King in 1886 and gave birth to Eugenia King in 1890. A resident of Bridge Street, she died on April 5, 1937.

This picture of the King family was taken at the King home on Bridge Street in 1899. Eugenia King is standing on the flower box. Behind her are her father, Dr. Frederick King, and her mother, Sarah Bostwick King.

# Six

# FARMING

The original owner of the Chapin farm on Chapin Road was Carl Lyons. The farm was started c. the 1800s. Charlie P. Chapin, grandfather of the Chapin family was born in 1862. He married Edith Amelia Lyons. In those years, the meadows were always dotted with cows. This photograph dates from the mid-1800s.

Sarah Morrisey Halpine was the grandmother of New Milford-born Betty Halpine and Stewart Francis Halpine, who became a town selectman.

J. Stuart Halpine was the grandfather of Stewart Francis Halpine and Betty Halpine of New Milford. This photograph was taken of at Christmastime in 1932.

Stewart Halpine had the largest tobacco farm in the Housatonic Valley in the 1930s. He is shown with young Stewart Francis Halpine and Betty Halpine in the garden. The house behind them is the Honeymoon Cottage at the Homestead Inn in New Milford.

Stewart Halpine leans forward, stacking the tobacco at his farm. The farm was the largest grower and packer of tobacco in the Housatonic Valley.

Alice Dickenson Halpine, left, wife of Steward Halpine, poses with her children Stewart Francis and Betty Halpine.

Young Stewart Francis Halpine sits astride the horse Pop Eyes, pulling the farm cart. This photograph was taken in 1932.

Phillip Hipp uses the manure spreader at the Hipp farm on Route 109 c. 1940.

At the Hipp farm on Route 109, Bill Hipp uses a machine that automatically pushes corn into the silo to store for fodder. This photograph was taken in the 1950s.

Phillip Hipp and Elizabeth Hipp gather up the hay at the Hipp farm in the 1930s.

Busy eating, the cow ignores not only the camera but also James Hipp and Margie Landry. This photograph was taken at the Hipp farm in 1938.

William Bostwick pauses as the cows wander in all directions along Park Lane. This photograph was taken looking south from the Bostwick Homestead in 1906. The old house was taken down c. 1906. The Howlands now own a home where the old house stood.

This is the Cobble Hill Dairy Farm, one of the last working farms in New Milford. Located on West Meetinghouse Road in the Merryall section of New Milford, the house was built by the Mr. Young who owned Young's Hotel on Richmond Street. The farm's present owners are Mr. and Mrs. Charles Flynn; they purchased it on July 4, 1955.

These buildings were at the Stack farm on Route 7. Robert Stack started farming in 1951. He ran the Stack farm as a milk farm. It is now a thing of the past. Today, only two working farms remain in the New Milford area.

At their home on Route 7, the Stack family share a happy moment. Glenys Stack and Robert Stack hold their 18-month-old son Robert Stack.

The Siskey farm was built in 1864 on Ridge Road. Loring Canfield was the original builder. The house contained wallpaper that dated from 1865, the year that Pres. Abraham Lincoln was assassinated.

The barns on Siskey farm were built in the 1700s on Old Ridge Road. They were first used as a blacksmith shop. The barns were destroyed in a fire.

The Reimeridge farm is located on Chapin Road. For many, many years it was a working farm. Its chief product was milk, and the cattle were Holstein cows.

At the Hipp farm, Grandpa Hipp, left, and another member of the Hipp family load the cart with trees cut down either for wood burning or fence building. The photograph was taken in the early 1900s.

# Seven
# A Look Around

This train wreck occurred at Merwinsville (now Gaylordsville) c. 1910.

The railroad station is shown in this photograph taken looking north from the intersection at Bridge Street c. 1920s.

A carload of coal and a caboose are at the end of a freight train on the tracks at the railroad station. The top of the freight house is visible at the right in this 1920s photograph.

This photograph of the old freight depot was taken between 1902 and 1906. Across the street is Golden's Store and Albert Evitt's drugstore, which was Botsford's in earlier days.

Parking space is pretty well taken up in this 1950s photograph of the railroad station.

Driving the Model T truck tha he remodeled for apple picking is Edward Howland, at the Wayside Fruit Gardens in 1936.

Truman Richmond, who had a passion for automobiles, sits in a 1932 Chevrolet. The picture was taken in Northville.

With a guard standing behind it, a school bus turns around on Bridge Street. This photograph was taken looking west across the railroad tracks. Notice the streetlights and the gatehouse on the right, past the tracks.

This was Cuddy's Gas Station on Bridge Street c. the 1950s. Notice the 1919 Model T Ford. The gas station is now a Citco station, owned by Graig and Raeanne Sansom.

Mr. Percy, right, is honored by the railroad for his 50 years of service in the late 1930s. On the left are employees of the New Milford Hat Company who are waiting for the train.

The gates are down at the Bridge Street railroad crossing. On the right in this 1930s photograph are the gatehouse and the Thomas F. Young House.

The race is on at the New Milford Fairgrounds Race Track, which was located at Fort Hill in the years from 1905 to 1910. These spectacular races drew large crowds.

Cows come around to the square on Old Park Lane. Today, this area is occupied by the New Milford Family Practice, at One Old Park Lane.

This photograph of Soule Brothers Tobacco was taken in c. 1886. Alfred Heacock, fifth from the left in the back row, was the shop foreman.

The New Milford Hat Company was located on Housatonic Avenue. Hats were manufactured there in the early 1900s. After the hat industry died out, the building became a fur-processing plant.

This view of the Still River and the valley beyond was taken from the bridge in 1898.

The building with a man standing in the front is Golden's Clothing Store. The picture was taken c. 1905 from the west side of Railroad Street opposite Bank Street.

The first gristmill was built in 1717 by John Griswald and William Gauld at Lanesville. This mill also served as a sawmill, a dam-bolting works, a clothes mill, and an ironworks. In May 1789, Capt. Joseph Ruggles purchased Eli Dunning's half of the ironworks at Lanesville; Ruggles died in 1802 at 71 years of age.

This March 1951 photograph shows Golden's Department Store on Bank Street. For many years the Goldens had a retailing business in New Milford.

The fire of 1902 destroyed the First National Bank building at the corner of Bank and Railroad Streets. The bank was moved to a new location.

This was the original fruit stand at Wayside Fruit Gardens at 43 Park Lane Road (Route 202), which opened in 1899. The owners were Edward Clyde Howland and his wife, Annie Bostwick Howland. By the 1930s, the stand had expanded and had become popular with visitors from New York City.

The fire of 1902 devastated the Main Street area of New Milford. Many buildings and businesses were lost.

The New Milford Bridge over the Housatonic River was under construction in 1953.

Ethel Worley, front center, was the daughter of Alfred C. Worley and Ada Worley, a family who had lived in New Milford since 1902. Her father bought the *Gazette* and the *New Milford Times*. In 1918, she married Percival Prince. Over the years, she was involved in many activities, such as the United Fund, the March of Dimes, and the Christmas lighting of the green. She was the founder of the Santa Claus Emergency Fund. She served on many town committees, including the Commission on Aging and the Board of Tax Review.

Howard H. Peck served as New Milford town clerk from 1938 to 1970. He was also the town historian. He was born on February 19, 1893, on Grove Street.

This baseball team played in the late 1800s. One member of the team has been identified: the late Judge John R. Addis, front row on the left.

The Boy Cadets pose in 1907 in front of the C.M. Beach Home. Among those pictured (mostly by last name only) in the front are Sergeant Breining, Couch, Lathrop, Kyle, Captain Rettalick, Draper, Greining, Moore, Corporal Boyton, Knowles, Green, Halpin, Bouton, Hine, Mullins, Bray, and Beck. In the middle are Caldwell, Wesley Parcells, Corporal Barker, Clank, Mulchy, Halpin, and Corporal Barton. In the back are Capt. Clifford Noble, Lieutenant Noble, Hunt, Stone, Connors, Law, flagbearer Marcy, Howard Peck, Parcells, Warner, Hunter, Lieutenant Canfield, and Sergeant Robertson.

In the 1920s, the building on the south side of the New Milford Police Station was W. Oliver's blacksmith and wheelwright shop. Neither the building nor the business still exists.

Pictured is a 1929 Chrysler four-door, on sale in 1929 for $85. The car was owned by Edward Howland.

This picture was taken at Lake Waraumaug in New Preston in the late 1800s. Pictured is Mary Doty Bostwick, holding the rope, and her daughter Mary Bostwick Berry in the boat the *Fuji Yama*.

The Bostwick family camps out on Lake Waraumaug in 1902. Millie and Molly Bostwick are in the carriage. Members of the Howland family camped with the Bostwicks. Property at that time sold for only $100 an acre.

The well-known New England House hotel played an active part in the social and business life of New Milford in the 19th century. It was destroyed in the fire of 1902. Notice the overhanging balcony.

Mr. and Mrs. Ares Burnett arrived in New Milford in 1865. They are the grandparents of Glenys Stack. Burnett Road is named after them. This photograph was taken in 1880.

This house shown on Park Lane, pictured in 1919, was later remodeled as a tavern. In 1948, the Old Tavern was owned by Herbert Williams and it later became the Old Pug Tavern. More recently, it was owned by Ralph Baldwin, Fred Berry, Tanno ?, and Herb Williams. Today it belongs to Dr. Kreiger.

Charles Marsh was raised in the Lanesville district, not far from the bridge that was later named for him: Marsh Bridge. He enlisted in the Union Army on October 21, 1861. For outstanding heroism in battle during the Civil War, he was awarded the Congressional Medal of Honor. He died of tuberculosis at the age of 27 in Pawling, New York.

Thomas M. Stack Jr. of New Milford was a sergeant in the Corps of Engineers 102. He served in the Infantry, 26th Yankee Division, in 1918. He is the grandfather of Robert Stack of the Stack farm on Route 7.

Robert Stack, the son of Robert and Glenys Stack and the great-grandson of Thomas M. Stack Jr., wears his great-grandfather's gas mask, helmet, and rifle. In 1991, Robert Stack received the Academic Excellence Presidential Award from Pres. George Bush.

Roger Sherman was the only signer in the 13 colonies of the four fundamental documents: the Articles of Association in 1774, the Declaration of Independence in 1776, the Articles of Confederation in 1777, and the U.S. Constitution in 1787.

This firehouse was decorated for the Firemen's Parade in 1900. This is the Water Witch Hose Company No. 2. Notice the dirt street. The building still stands on Church Street.

Posing for this 1916 photograph are Raymond Bostwick (holding his hand over his eyes), Mary Doty Bostwick, Sara King, Jet (standing and facing sideways), Harriet (in the black hat), Mrs. Emmons (eating watermelon), Annie Howland, Lottie (peeking over Will's shoulder) Will, and Dr. Frederick King (looking up and wearing a black suit).

Mary Bostwick Berry, wife of Fred Berry, wears an elegantly styled dress. She lived on Park Lane.

This man standing at the Merwinsville Hotel on Forge Road in Gaylordsville is believed to be a Merwin. The woman is unidentified.

Pictured is Marjorie Merwin. The photograph was taken in the 1920s.

The Boardman Bridge was built in 1888. Notice the man on the top of the bridge and, third from the right, the man in a carriage.

This is the new bridge over Housatonic River—the Lover's Leap area. Notice the homes in the background.

The Lover's Leap Bridge is a well-known spot in New Milford.

This photograph of the Still River was taken from Lover's Leap c. the 1890s.

Pictured c. the 1890s is the Falls Bridge at Lover's Leap.

This photograph of the Still River was taken c. the 1890s from the riverbed by the bridge at Lover's Leap.

These two photographs taken c. the 1890s show the falls at Lover's Leap.

The legend is that the daughter of the Indian chief became attracted to a young white man and he to her. The match not being acceptable to the old chief, the lovers threw themselves off the point of rocks into the river and from this came Lover's Leap.

This 1890s photograph shows the cove at Lover's Leap.

A party was held at North Kent in 1898. Dr. Frederick King leads the families, who are related. Pictured with King are Lottie and Raymond Bostwick, Eugenia King, Sarah King, Mary Doty Bostwick (wearing a white apron), Edgar Bostwick (carrying the box), Dewitt King, William Bostwick, and Em and Lottie Bostwick (in back).

www.ingramcontent.com/pod-product-compliance
Lightning Source LLC
Chambersburg PA
CBHW080903100426
42812CB00007B/2143